THE
ART DECO MANSION
IN ST LUCIA

What drove the man who built it?

Ruth Bonetti

WORDS & *Music*

The Art Deco Mansion in St Lucia: What drove the man who built it?

© Ruth Bonetti 2021
Published by: Words and Music
PO Box 422
The Gap Qld. 4061 Australia
Mobile (+61) 0411 782 404
http://www.ruthbonetti.com

ISBN: 978-0-9875442-6-1

A catalogue record for this book is available from the National Library of Australia

Photo credits: Eric Back (p49, p78); Ruth Bonetti (p 10, p104); Brisbane City Council Archives website (Title page BCC-B54-1976; pp 22, 69, 94, 112); Fryer library, University of Queensland; *Flood damage at St Lucia, January 1974*, © State Library of Queensland/Author unknown; State Library of Queensland: Negative 177196p (p154); UQ (p134) from https://library-brisbane.ent.sirsidynix.net.au/client/en_AU/search/asset/16040/0. Maps courtesy of Michael Bretherton.

All rights reserved. No part of this publication may be reproduced, stored in a retrieval system or transmitted in any form by any means without the prior permission of the copyright owner. Enquiries should be made to the publisher.

This book is copyright. Apart from any fair dealing for the purposes of private study, research, criticism or review as permitted under the Copyright Act, no part of this book may be reproduced by any process without the written permission of the publisher.

DEDICATION

For Michael Bryce AM, AE. Vale.

Jane Bartlett

For those who also lived in the Art Deco mansion,
and enlarged on my childhood memories:

Jack Bryce
Cousins Jenny, John, Kay, Betty, Bob and Julie.

The Art Deco Mansion in St Lucia:
What drove the man who built it?

⇒ CONTENTS ⇐

Foreword by Kay Maxwell	9
Foreword by Jenny Starky	11
Prologue	13
Coronation Park Ltd	17
Doldrums	19
The Hunt for Plans	23
The Elevator	27
The Back Story	31
What Propelled Emigration?	33
Art Deco	37
Australia's Richest Finn	39
The 'Big House' Lounge Room	46
Further Back	47
The Munsala Milieu of WA Back's Upbringing	52
Arrival in Sydney, January 1903	54
Marriage 1908	57
A Gift of Music	59
The Mooball Home	63
The Sheep's Back	67
Early St Lucia	71
Set back: World War 1	75
Another Set Back: Spanish Influenza	79

Deliverance	86
Resumption of Land	87
Set Back: The Depression	93
Obstacles into Opportunities	97
The University of Queensland I	99
Opportunities — Yet Obstacles	101
Hazelwood *and* **Wilfred Downs**	105
The Wondrous Telephone	107
Tyranny of Distance from New South Wales	109
The 'Big House'	113
Stylish Bedrooms	117
Bathroom	119
The 'Roof Garden'	120
Hawken Drive Village	121
Getting an Education	127
University of Queensland II	131
Women in the Workplace — a Forward Thinker	135
Benefactor or a Soft Touch?	145
Patriarch and Family Man	147
A Man of Faith	151
Drought and Flooding Rains	155
1974 Floods	157
Do it Now	159
Grandma Christina Back	161
Dark Days of Dementia	162
Big House for Sale	167
Weddings and Funerals	169
A Last Word	173
What Drove the Man Who Built the 'Big House'?	177

Bibliography	*181*
Index of Names	*187*
Acknowledgments	*193*
About the Author	*195*
Other Books by Ruth Bonetti	*197*

FOREWORD

THE ELEGANT AND MYSTERIOUS post-war art deco mansion at Hawken Drive, St. Lucia is a much admired local landmark in the gracious, tree-lined, University suburb that lies comfortably in a bend of the Brisbane River. Generations of residents and visitors have passed by, wondering how it came to be, who owned it, who lived there, and feeling, perhaps, a twinge of envy in their musings.

The house was the brainchild of one of St. Lucia's most prominent early residents and a developer of the suburb, Swedish-Finn immigrant, Wilhelm Anders Back. WA, as he was known, emigrated to Australia in the early part of the 20th century and proceeded to build a business empire of rural, commercial, and residential property and associated pursuits. While growing his business interests, he also grew a large and talented Australian family and wide circle of international friends through his support of the wool industry, the arts, his church and a life-long and extensive commitment to charitable endeavours.

My mother, Joan Maxwell, was private secretary to WA Back from 1940 until his death in 1974. She adored WA and was forever grateful for his friendship, his mentoring and the opportunity to develop her career and complete further studies at a time when married women were largely confined to the home.

The Back family and the house at St. Lucia are central to my childhood memories. The house was like a fairyland to me.

While my mother worked, I explored and played in the vast and magical gardens, venturing into the house to chat with Mrs Back and Maria and pleading to ride the lift to the roof terrace and the glorious panoramic views across the river. Precious memories.

This wonderful book pays tribute to a home, a suburb, a family and the man who created it all.

–Kay Maxwell, LLB, Grad Dip Leg Prac, LLM, MEd

FOREWORD

I AM THE ELDEST OF William and Christina's twenty-four grandchildren. As such I was privileged to know our grandparents for a little longer time than the other grandchildren and also had their full attention—although we lived many miles apart—for almost two years until my brother came into the world. Soon the family increased to the cheers of our grandfather. He dreamed of having one hundred family members, the Back family's effort at populating Australia in the middle of the twentieth century.

Our Grandad, as he was affectionately known to us, was many things to many people but above all he was a family man. Often he related that, when he was engaged to marry Christina and had planned their home on a farm being established on virgin land, he realised that the land would not be as fertile as he had expected. That the earning capacity was not sufficient to keep a wife in the manner that he hoped was so devastating that he talked about it for the rest of his life. I believe that the reason he had comfortable homes through the years was because he wanted to provide well for his family.

My Grandparents, and their second son Elwyn with a wife and four children, moved into the Art Deco house on Hawken Drive in late 1951. This was exciting for the children who came from a very different environment in hot, dry far central-western Queensland. Landscaping was not an industry then and my Grandfather was frustrated when he sent a man to buy plants and he returned with a handful of little seedlings and not much else. Our Grandmother and my mother loved a garden and so it gradually grew.

We are fortunate to have had grandparents who made themselves available to so many of us and made each individual feel that he or she was the most important one of the bunch. Grandad was the solid rock of our large family, the person we looked up to because he gave consideration to the varied decisions everybody must make. He had ideas for renovating a building or financing the purchase of a mob of cattle, as well as advice to one of his grandsons about investing in a certain sheep station. He was always looking after the spiritual lives of those around him. My father would remind us that Grandad would give sound advice on suitable grazing country because he had learnt those lessons the hard way. Grandma was the kind, gentle lady who kept the home life ticking over.

I have an image in my head of the sad grandparents in front of the Hawken Drive house, seventy years ago, saying goodbye to our family when we were leaving for our western Queensland home for a school holiday. They prayed for our safety, waved and said, 'Drive carefully over the bad stretches and take it slowly.'

–Jenny Starky

PROLOGUE

'Penny a look!'

My brothers were not shy about accosting the ogle-eyed residents of St Lucia loitering near the unfinished Art Deco mansion. As it rose from foundations to scaffolding to four-level glory, the boys perched on the brick pillars of its fence and listened to the murmurs.

'Tsk, tsk, such a lavish house for the post-war building restrictions.'

It was unusual for a private residence to have an elevator so the boys found it easy to make fun of the gawking burghers of 1950s Brisbane. The entrepreneurial spirit so evident in their grandfather was not lost in them as they spotted an opportunity to use his building project for their own benefit.

What drove the man whose vision led to a landmark icon of St Lucia, and who developed a southern swathe of the suburb?

His eldest son Eric Back wrote of the opposition and controversy to such a Big House:

> Dad assured the authorities he had the material; he was bringing it from New South Wales. He took a lot of stopping when he decided what he wanted.

Grandad built his first St Lucia house at 160 Highland Terrace, while planning his mansion at 209 Hawken Drive. He said, 'We'll throw a shilling into the cement mix for good luck.' Building materials were at a premium after World War II; as soldiers were demobilised so the demand for low cost housing rose. Post-war building materials were stretched and restrictions on size tight.

WA argued that this mansion would house two families; their second son Elywn, his wife Joan and their family of Jennifer (Jenny), Bob, Betty and Dawn, joined him and Grandma for education at Ironside State School. Like his father, Elwyn was always busy. And like other country mothers, Joan had struggled to juggle correspondence lessons while running a household and property. After moving into the 'Big House' in Hawken Drive, she ran that household and Grandad gave our family long-term use of this earlier home nearby at 160 Highland Terrace.

A glossy PR brochure touts the features of the 'Big House' with a view to selling it in the mid-1960s. It is classic realtor language:

A glimpse of the lovely lounge room and (inset) the automatic lift which provides effortless access to all floors and the roof garden area.

> Availability of this magnificent dwelling...
> one of Brisbane's foremost luxury homes...
> provides an unprecedented opportunity to purchase
> a residence which combines the unusual in design
> with truly extraordinary practical advantages.
> It is situated only five miles from the heart
> of the city in a pre-eminent locality, on three
> allotments (66 perches) of land with the frontage
> of 142'6". Set in beautifully kept terraced lawns
> and gardens, the building ensures maximum privacy
> while commanding fascinating glimpses and full
> panoramic views of some of Brisbane's finest
> city, river and mountain scenery.
>
> Construction is in reinforced concrete and brick
> on three floor levels with a total of fourteen
> rooms. There is also a spacious roof garden area
> and excellent accommodation for three cars.[2]

Taking the lift down to the basement we slide the grille doors and enter a spooky, dark space, with roaring air conditioning noise and fractured light through textured glass bricks. There was a security safe and carpentry workshop with lathe; Grandad worked with wood since his youth in Finland. This was the office in the early days, before one was built at the bottom of the garden. Cousins John and Bob built a gun in that room, with a string to fire it around the corner. A bullet hole still commemorates their air-rifle building escapade.

> Facilities on the lower ground floor include a maid's
> room with bathroom... a roomy office with built-
> in strong-room... laundry... machinery room...
> storeroom... and a separate shower and toilet.

The laundry included one of the earliest automated washing machines, which cousin Jenny notes 'took a long time to do a cycle.' But it was a move forward from the rub board, dolly tub, copper, mangle and wash board.

Beside another photograph we read:

```
Conveniently grouped on the ground floor are
the dining room, complete with craftsman-built
suite, wall-to-wall carpeting, venetian blinds
and curtains... a writing room. Toilet facilities
are also located on this floor. The lounge room
also with high-quality suite and wall-to-wall
carpeting...
```

I remember high ceilings, dark Chinoiserie wallpaper, Venetian blinds and heavy drapes against the Queensland sun. An opulent carpet. The marble statues. The red brocade arm chair in which Grandad rocked me while singing a Swedish nursery rhyme.

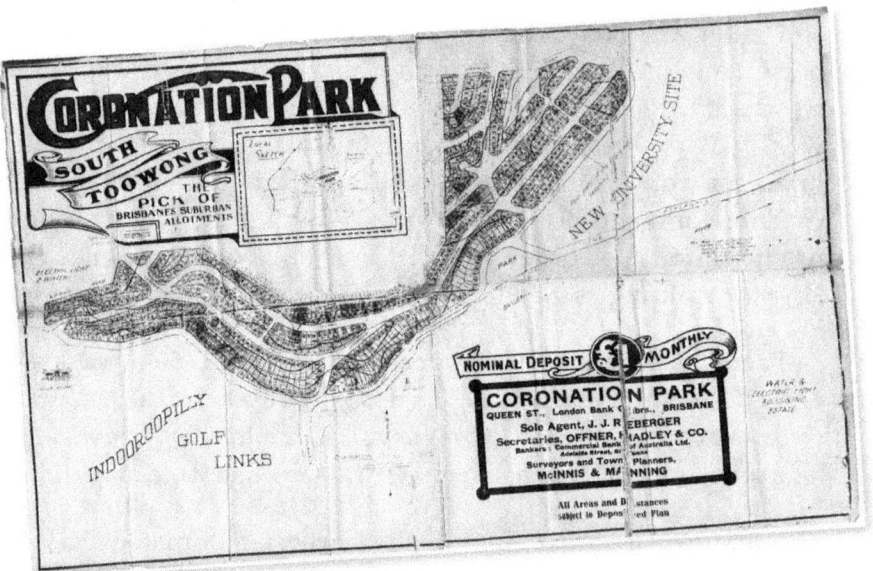

⇒ CORONATION PARK LTD ⇐

The Coronation Park story began in May 1922 when a syndicate of graziers and business people bought 148 acres on terms from The National Bank of Australasia. The Company, Coronation Park Ltd, was set up with a capital structure of 50,000 shares at £1/-/- each, by a firm of solicitors who, to get the company registered, used six staff names purchasing one share each. Soon after fourteen other persons made substantial purchases of shares. It would appear that only these 9,857 shares were sold, and all were held until voluntary liquidation. (State Archives microfilm Z3977 p 156 and File A/28567)

That year, two large subdivisions were made at St. Lucia—one by Coronation Park Ltd., the other, St Lucia Heights, by T. M. Burke Pty. Ltd. Roads followed the contours of the hills, which would reduce as far as possible the steepness of the grades. Coronation Drive and Highland Terrace are excellent examples of roads following hill contours and avoiding steep climbs. On a clear day a person possessing good eyesight could tell the time from the City Hall clock. (*The Courier Mail*, 26 February 1936)

In 1922 the name Coronation Park was adopted by a private company syndicate that developed around 15% of the suburb St Lucia. It appears to have been headed by WA Back, dubbed by some as 'a father of St Lucia' who drew together a team of loyal supporters from hubs of Mullumbimby and Brisbane.

The Doyle family contributed 4,500 shares. E J Doyle, a grazier from Longreach in Western Queensland, owned 2,500 shares.

Edward Joseph Doyle, who died in 1968, was the second son of the Irish immigrant, John Christopher Doyle. EJ's father came from Tambo and died on 8 October 1908. Besides Edward, the other Doyle siblings—Peter, Patrick, Mary Ellen and Henry—bought 2,000 shares. Beyond this start-up they appear to have been sleepers in the consortium until EJ Doyle was listed as a director when the company went into voluntary receivership.

Other leaders in the investment with 1000 shares each were:

- WA Back, grazier
- G Mallum, Mullumbimby Storekeeper.

With 500 shares each:

- GF Offner, Auchenflower Accountant
- VJ Offner, Valley Storekeeper
- MM Tierney (Ms), Lismore Nurse
- JH Carmichael, Brisbane Company Manager
- GE Ashbury, Mullumbimby Postmaster.

The consortium also included C Seamens, a Sydney Traveller (300 shares); McInnis and Manning, Brisbane Surveyors (250 shares). With 100 shares each were:

- Baker and Nicol, Brisbane Sales Managers
- EV Nelson, a Mullumbimby Clerk who managed WA's business office for 56 years from 1920)
- Nurse CA Henry of Gympie. Nurse Henry had a long relationship with the Back family since she was engaged to care for WA's young daughter Gloria when she was frail; she changed Gloria's intake from cow to goat's milk.

The Coronation Park Estate was opened in 1923 by the then Governor of Queensland (Sir Matthew Nathan), who, an engineer himself, praised the layout (*The Sunday Mail*, 18 February, 1940) to reduce the steepness of the grades. This was one of the civic triumphs of Mr RA McInnes, who was to become town planner of Brisbane.

In 1925, the first Lot sale was recorded on the Title, but only fourteen more occurred during the first year, in Portions 19–25. Indeed, the next ten years saw only a further seventy sales.

Grandad aimed high. However, the times were agiainst his Brisbane Coronation Park project.

DOLDRUMS

Eldest son Eric Back wrote about the St Lucia development in his memoir:

> The purchase price was to be about £24,000. The land included [part of] the (now) Indooroopilly Golf Club, then along the river to include a lot of the University grounds, but away from the frontage it was mostly undeveloped bush.

By 1926 few other blocks were sold or built on. That year, Professor Melbourne pursued a scheme for the University to buy much more land in St Lucia. Eventually 200 blocks for the colleges mainly in Portions 17 and 18 and the south-east corner of Portion 19, were resumed by Brisbane City Council in 1926. (Cited by Peter Brown, *Residential Development after the 1880s*, St Lucia History Group Paper No 11, 2017.)

In 1933, the company name was changed to Coronation Park Pty Ltd.

When the syndicate went into voluntary liquidation in 1945–6, assets exceeded liabilities and some monies were returned to shareholders. The Directors who formally applied for the liquidation were Messrs EJ Doyle, WA Back, GF Offner, and VJ Offner.

WA Back was left with a parcel of land to develop and sell. He commuted from his Northern Rivers office in Mullumbimby until relocating to Brisbane in September 1949. He had already built his office in 128 Highland Terrance, and a home at 160 Highland Terrace. Meanwhile, he planned an innovative landmark mansion.

For the next nine years Coronation Park Ltd watched as disaster and near bankruptcy took over. Many of the blocks were passed back to the sub-dividers or were sold for unpaid rates.

To most observers this looked like the end of St Lucia... to most that is except Mr Back and his partners. 'From the time I first saw the beautiful hills of St Lucia I knew that one day it would blossom,' Grandad mused at one point. 'There were times though, that courage, faith—and a bundle of unwanted land—was all that we had. The subdivision had been carried out on a contour town plan system by two of the best surveyors in the business [McInnis and Manning]. We wanted to make it a model suburb; and even in the early days each sale contract carried certain development clauses.' (*The Telegraph*, 25 January p 33 c 3.)

St Lucia was just easing out of the economic doldrums when World War II—and the consequent building restrictions—struck another blow to progress.

They acquired 148 acres—representing the best land in the district—and converted it into 870 lush building blocks from dairy land and scrub.

Eric wrote that:

> Blocks of land were advertised for £10 deposit and £1 monthly with water and electricity. All might have gone well for Coronation Park if the Depression had not arrived soon after it started. People may have paid a few pounds' deposit on a block but then when they got their rates from the Council, they mostly forfeited the land as the best way out. Certainly no one could build in those days.

The 1894 Certificate of Title for the estate is partially damaged but does not seem to confirm the above. The overall Title remained with the Bank, with individual Lots sold off between 1925 and 1945, when the remaining blocks, some 28 acres, were transferred to Coronation Park Pty Ltd. (Certificate of Title No. 142780.) No mortgages are recorded. It is possible that prior to 1945 the syndicate had a business arrangement with the bank where the syndicate acted as developer but the bank retained ownership. When the blocks were sold, the funds from the sale could have been split between the bank and the developer. This is a common practice even today.

The two main estates were subdivided by different surveyors, and that has resulted in a problem of conflicting roadways in some sections. The subdivision of Coronation Park was one of the first civic triumphs of Mr. R. A. McInnes, who was now town planner of Brisbane.

SURVEY AND ... PLANNING FILE NUMBER							
ROAD	HAWKEN DRIVE						
		Utte		20 1'Pkwy			
AREA							
0.040							
SPECIAL RESTRICTIONS	Health Dept Hawaii 27.6.93 1'10'2 Sewage disposal by ...						
1st CLASS 1 STOREY	be not 15.7.33						
	let with						
OWNERSHIP	PRIVATE COUNCIL STATE ...						
SERVICES AVAILABLE	ROAD WATER SEWERAGE ELECT GAS						
	RECORD OF CITY APPLICATIONS						
DATE MINUTE SUB DETAIL APPLICANT ...			REMARKS	FEE No			

UPIN | 209 - A 4708 | 661 |

SITE APPROVED FOR SEPTIC TANK DATE 5.4.-4 MINUTE 23315 REMARKS 50'x 1'9" x 2' subject ... absorption trench not less than ...

THE HUNT FOR PLANS

LITTLE IS KNOWN OF THE HOUSE provenance except that *The Sunday Mail* on 17 June 1951 noted the building contractors were E.R. Cramphorn and N. Millin, who believed it would be the most modern house in Brisbane. At just over 2000 square feet, the house would contain ten rooms. (General limit for a house was 1250 square feet.) Bricks for the house came from Coombell, near Casino; the timber from Mullumbimby, cement from Britain and Sweden, and the steel from Japan. It described 'Hustling, stocky wool baron, Mr. W. A. Back' and noted his lifetime with sheep and cattle, and interest in sheep properties in Queensland ranging from 20,000 acres to the 303 square mile *Aberfoyle* station on Torrens Creek, 240 miles west of Mackay.

At the Brisbane City Council Archives, I located a microfilm that notes a septic tank was approved for the site on 5 September 1949 and building permission on 19 October 1949.

Perhaps Grandad located designs for the 'Big House' in America. Eric writes that they 'took off in 1950 with letters of introduction to Boston wool firms.'

The Mullumbimby Star tracked his May 1950–January 1951 travels overseas, during which time he may have absorbed Art Deco architecture:

31 May 1950:   W. A. Back in USA and will leave for Finland shortly.

27 June 1950:   Mr and Mrs E. J. Holm Anna Sanna née Back of Billinudgel celebrated their golden wedding anniversary. Telegram from Mrs Holm's brother Mr W. A. Back in New York.

12 January 1951: W. A. Back returned from overseas. Is building a £25,000 mansion in St Lucia.

Subsequent owners were Michael and Quentin Bryce, the first woman to become Governor-General of Australia. Michael Bryce put unsuccessful efforts into finding architectural plans for the Art Deco mansion. During his years at 160 Highland Terrace, WA Back lived next door to respected architect Ronald Voller. If only he had called on him to design the 'Big House', layout flaws might have been averted.

Eric Back bemoaned in his Memoir:

> It was as solid as the Rock of Gibraltar, but I think that an architect should have been consulted. At least he may have noticed the stairs and lift were too small to take the furniture up to the top floor. They had to get a crane to lift it on the outside.

From 1981 until the 1990s Jack Bryce enjoyed his guy cave downstairs in a suite which contained an office with the strong room vault in it. There was also a maid's room and bathroom. His hide-out must have been a boys' own world. Jack noted:

> 'The rooms were not large for the entertaining my parents did. It had a major renovation a few years ago—I think that opened up interior spaces—the challenge in renovating is to keep heritage-listed character features.'

There were parties and photo shoots on the roof deck. 'The challenge was getting everyone up and down with narrow stairs and lift.'

He appreciated the 'sense of strength and quality with details such as curved glass window, timber wall panelling, the elevator with chrome features.'

To me as a child, the house was enormous. Decades later when I visited the 'Big House' as an adult, it had shrunk. Michael Bryce offered me a guided tour of the house just before they sold it. As we walked towards the front door, he pointed to the adjacent carport on the right.

'We painted over that Alpine fresco on the side, it didn't fit with the Art Deco Style.'

'Giuseppe Ive painted the fresco. His wife Maria did some domestic cleaning, and they may have lived in the maid's quarters. He studied art in Italy but now worked as a house painter.' I agree the frescoes are little loss though the scene of white-capped mountains rising out of flowered meadows stirred my urge to travel. I had read the *Heidi* books many times.

'The choice of scene made the owner a likely European. Swiss, or Scottish perhaps?'

'Grandad named the house *Munsala*, after his home village in Finland.'

If Michael Bryce, a respected architect and designer had no idea of the house's heritage, after assiduous research, who could know? I determined to tell the story about the man who built an elevator in his house.

THE ELEVATOR

Michael Bryce opened the door and there in front of me—for the first time since childhood—I saw the famous lift. Imagine a man building an elevator in a private home! It was such an eyebrow-lifting thought that, when I attended Ironside State School, I was dubbed 'the granddaughter of the man who built a lift in his house.'

It was one of those old-fashioned elevators with accordion-style doors that, if left open, would not respond to button-pressing until they were clicked shut. Grandma, increasingly forgetful as dementia encroached on her mind, would leave the doors open on an upper level, rendering the lift inoperative. Grandad had the foresight to include an intercom system that connected the basement, ground floor and the first floor.

Real estate advertising in the 1970s proclaimed:

```
All floors are fully AIR-CONDITIONED...
serviced by an AUTOMATIC ELEVATOR and linked with
a highly efficient INTERCOMMUNICATION SYSTEM.
```

All very modern, Grandad. Your vision was ahead of your time.

Those curved glass sliding doors with leaf pattern encrusted on, in an era of box-rectangle or square houses. The green glass bricks in the lounge, stairwell, bathroom and basement would be difficult to make or replace. The lower floor gloom was illumined by a whole window of these textured glass bricks.

Curves were pivotal to the design, built around the air-conditioner. A plate in the basement notes it was built in 1952, a *'Carrier Weather Maker'* reverse cycle. It still works as experts are excited to see.

What was the source of Grandad's inspiration? Was he fascinated to ride an elevator in Finland, an innovation that had just come to the Stockmann Department Store in Helsinki before he emigrated on 26 November 1902?

From the entrance, we turn left into the lounge room, and I swirl down a time warp to the red velvet armchair and into Grandad's portly lap. His lilting Swedish accent croons into my memories:

Rida rida Ranka, hästen heter Blanka
Vart ska vi rida? Till en liten piga
Vad kan hon heta? Jungfru Margareta
den tjocka och den feta.

Ride, ride a rocking horse, the horse's name is Blanka.
Where shall we ride? To a little girl.
What is her name? The Virgin Margareta
The chubby and the fat one.

His knee becomes the rocking horse. At the end of the ditty, his knees separate to deliver little Ruth onto the carpet. Sixty years later, the song revives in Brisbane as I sing my grandsons to sleep in my rocking chair.

Did I sing it to my own sons? This nursery rhyme skipped a generation, and evolved some odd nuances. I sang it to colleagues when my husband and I lived two years in Sweden. Their polite bemusement told me my inflections had added risqué improvisations. After visiting the family home, I can envisage my great-grandmother singing it to her children.

Grandad's childhood in Finland was enriched by this and other stories from the *Reading for Children* volumes, published between 1847 and 1896. The author Zacharias Topelius was born in 1818 on the family farm, Kuddnäs near Nykarleby, just ten kilometres away from Grandad's hometown of Munsala.

Swedish accent? Didn't you say your grandfather was a Finn?

As we tour the now not-so-Big House, I tell Michael some of Grandad's heritage.

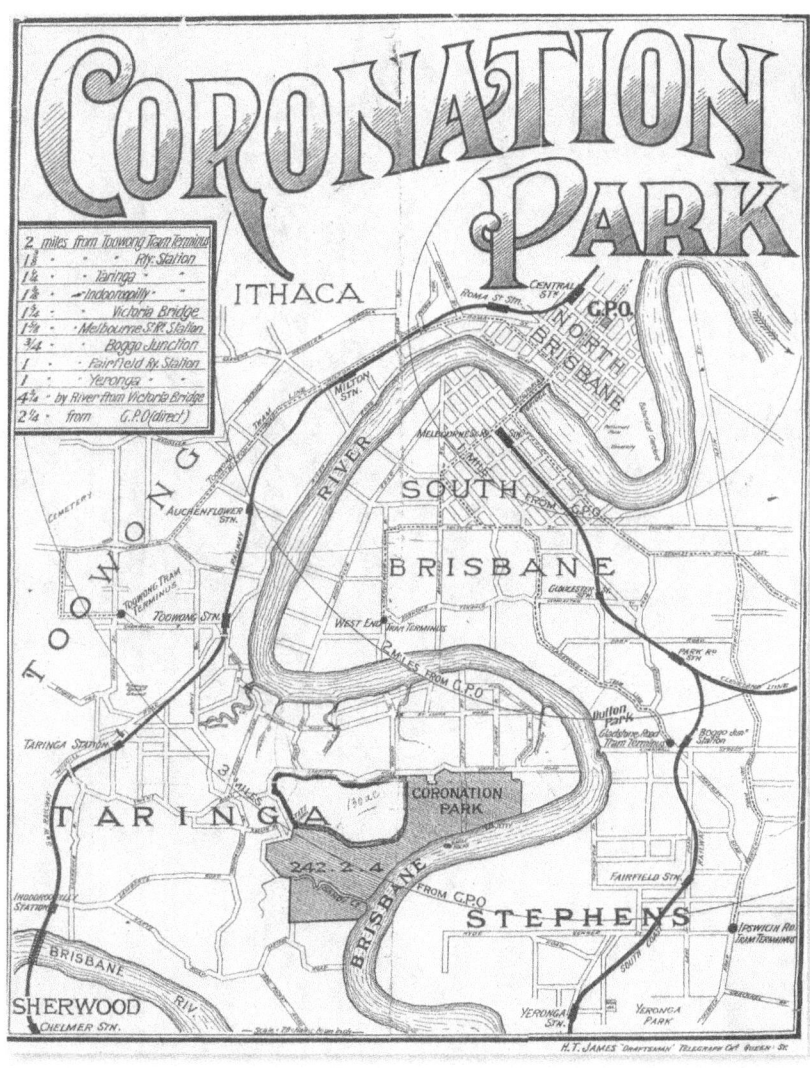

THE BACK STORY

MEET THE MAN WHOSE VISION and taste built the St Lucia Art Deco house, William Andrew Back. In Swedish, his native language, Wilhelm Anders Back. Sometimes called Will or Billy Back and more often, WA.

Grandad was born on 29 July 1886 in Munsala, a small but important village in Ostrobothnia, Finland on the west coast. This was settled by Swedes, hence Swedish culture and language.

The family on both sides of the globe were prolific letter writers. Just as well, for any genealogist or historian who types 'Back' into a search engine will be frustrated by links to 'back row' and 'full back'. WA proves elusive to track in print.

Grandad loved the camera, but more to send photographs back home than for publicity. He appears to have shied away from that, though presentation was paramount—as his evolving business letterheads attest.

He ran a busy office, firstly at 37 The Esplanade, St Lucia, and also at Dell Road in the same suburb.

Grandad wrote to his Finnish family on 28 April 1971:

> This business keeps the books for all those different properties and different members of the groups.
>
> It is a very big job for this office, as there are 84 different Income Tax Returns now to attend to, apart from all the other business attached to all those different properties and different members of the group. So this office is becoming very important.
>
> Apart from Mr Vincent Nelson who has been with me 50 years we have his son now, David Nelson, taking up the threads and of course Joan Maxwell has been with me nearly 30 years since about 14 years of age. Then we have Miss Colleen Nelson, on the bookkeeping, which is a constant job to write up all the books for the different members.
>
> [Daughter] Gloria's husband Victor Houseman also has an office and is working in conjunction with these other four members.

Generations of Swedes named SONS after their fathers and grandfathers so family trees sprout bewildering repetitions. Our tribe typifies this: Olof Olofsson Ohls was mentioned in parish records in 1577, and such names multiplied amid an occasional Johansson and Johansdotter. Nine generations later, Grandad's grandfather (my 'farfar-farfar' as the Swedish language gives an admirable system to track relatives) broke the mould as Karl Andersson Back.

While studying music at University of Queensland, I attempted to adopt Bach. But in Swedish Back means *a little hill*, as opposed to Johann Sebastian's *little brook*. The bland name provided sanctuary during world wars when foreign names, distinguished by the likes of umlauts, caused suspicion—and even internment.

WHAT PROPELLED EMIGRATION?

The Swedish-speaking west coast of Finland was a hub of activism and resistance to the Russian oppression. This escalated after the Tsar refused to receive a five-hundred-man delegation who bore a petition with half a million signatures. This period of the First Oppression triggered a rush of migration between 1899 and 1905. At its peak in 1902, the year Grandad left the country, 23,000 registered as emigrants.

Grandad and his black sheep brother Karl Johan (known as KJ) emigrated to Australia to avoid conscription into the Russian army. The Back brothers—or their father—chose well. It turned out that Australia was the only country to hold a referendum—twice—that allowed men to choose to fight, rather than tolerate conscription.

As a Grand Duchy under Russia, Finland enjoyed relative peace until Tsar Nicholas II broke his coronation vow to retain the freedoms Finns had enjoyed for 90 years. Instead, in autumn 1898, he appointed Governor General Nikolai Bobrikov, who had orders to Russianise them. The Tsar gave Bobrikov unlimited power over the Finns—and that included a conscription edict to serve for five years in the Russian army.

Bobrikov overrode the Finnish parliament with a manifesto that asserted Russian rule and violated their constitution. The First Era of Oppression dictated that the Lutheran church—already vulnerable to Pietist and Baptist popularity—must bow to the Russian Orthodox religion. Russian language, currency and stamps must be used.

In 1899, Grandad's older brother Karl Johan Back was indeed balloted and called up for service in the armed forces. He fled. At Suez Canal, Russian military police boarded his ship and asked for him. His nephew Rolf Back quoted to me his words, 'If they find me I swim to shore and take my chances with the Arabs'. A friend's passport allowed 'KJ' to dodge their surveillance, and he settled in the Byron Bay hinterland.

The plans for his younger brother to follow him were knotted out through letters and in family 'congerichuchans' from the time Wilhelm was ten.

Grandad's secretary Joan Maxwell heard him tell the story many times. She quoted it in her *OBITUARY—MEMORIAL MINUTES:*

'Tourism was not promoted or popular information was scant. Find out the best way you could. Stroll around the wharves and shipping offices in the Baltic Seaside ports and towns. Talk with the sailors and sea going folk, some must be sure to talk. Evidently, some did. Questions asked and answered. Canada was spoken of as too bleak, too cold. USA as prosperous, much strife, and negro problem. New Zealand, too many earthquakes. What about Australia? Dry, arid, bush fires, some parts all right, such as the eastern coast. Cape Byron had the highest rainfall, the best country is at the most easterly point. Right, let us try it.'

For, as my father's cousin Rolf told in his Swedish accent, 'Anders Back directed KJ to head for the most easterly point; for there must be rain.'

Finland around the turn of the 19th to 20th centuries was a dark, oppressed vassal nation under Russia. When my husband Antoni and I lived two years in Sweden, directly across the Gulf of Bothnia from Munsala, Grandad's birthplace, we soon understood the endless long winters; one white and one green. But who could comprehend the oppressive Russian regime without living through it?

ART DECO

Why did WA Back choose to build his mansion in Art Deco style?

Cousin John Back suggests that when, in 1946–47, the Coronation Park Ltd company wound up voluntarily and the unsold land was divided among the partners, WA Back was left with a parcel of about 40 blocks. He also agreed to take over the sale of some of the other land of his associates. 'With post-war housing shortages,' John says, 'St Lucia was growing into a hobo town, as anyone could put up a shack. WA envisaged a suburb of class. He set an example that others followed.'

'In 1948 there were mobs of kangaroos all over the place, dirt roads, and no worthwhile shopping facilities,' Grandad said. (*The Telegraph,* 25 January 1962 p 33 c 3.) He built several houses as a 'booster'. Meaning that he hoped to inspire other potential home-owners to follow his lead.

Art Deco was known in Sweden and Finland as *funkis* for functionalism. The style was pioneered in the Turku area of Finland from early 1930s. Originally known as 'style moderne' until the 1960s, it embraced technologies of the future after the grim years of World War 1. The 'roaring twenties' flappers kicked up their short skirts and heels in a new world of freedom, innovation and luxury. In 1925, the Musée des Arts Décoratifs in Paris introduced to the world an Exhibition of Modern Decorative and Industrial Arts 'to keep alive in France the culture of the arts which seek to make useful things beautiful.'

That year, F. Scott Fitzgerald embodied the era in his novel *The Great Gatsby.*

Art Deco architecture featured sleek geometric designs using man-made materials such as concrete, glass and terrazzo floors. Large windows, flat roofs and corner curves eschewed fussy ornamentation for understated chevrons and geometric patterns.

The Brisbane City Council citation dated February 2011 reads:

> Constructed in 1950, this is an excellent example of a Functionalist/Art Deco styled house, arguably one of the best examples in Brisbane. This house has an original lift, which is a rarity for any house in Brisbane, and certainly rare for a house of this age. The house is a local landmark, owing to its prominent height and distinctive features.
>
> The design of the house features strong horizontal lines typical of the Modern Movement as it was known in Australia in the 1930s and 40s. This horizontality is achieved in this design in its capped parapet, flat cantilevered concrete window hoods, and solid balustrade over the entry. Modern features also include the streamlined corners, and steel framed casement windows. Art Deco features include the semi-circular swept parapet line on the lift tower combined with the porthole window, the stripped classical columns around the entry and the crisp geometric mouldings of the parapet.
>
> The place is important because of its aesthetic significance as an excellent example of a private home executed in the Functionalist/Art Deco style in Brisbane and which has become a local landmark... demonstrating a high degree of creative or technological achievement at a particular period.
>
> An excellent example of the Functionalist/Art Deco style and a notable building in the pattern of twentieth century Brisbane architecture.

AUSTRALIA'S RICHEST FINN

Heading up a consortium from its inception in 1921, through the downward spiral of the Depression, World War II and its aftermath, cast a burden on WA Back's shoulders. I only realised the heavy impact on his own health and mind when my Finnish family gave me a copy of a two-page colour article from an unnamed Finnish magazine article. The author is not acknowledged, and it is undated but probably published in 1963 or '64. This gave fresh insights and an overview of the life of an extraordinary *'Migrant Made Good.'*

> The richest and the most successful Finn lives in Brisbane, at least that is where his house and office are located. He spends most of his time in Brisbane, unless he needs to catch his private plane to oversee his sheep and the 200,000 hectares of farmland. From his office he manages 20 different farms remotely. When you've had the kind of success that William Andrew Back has had, you've made it. Even if you don't know him by name, in Brisbane you will be able to find his place by asking for a man who has his own lift in his house.
>
> Despite knowing where his house was located I didn't want to rush over there. Instead I asked pastor Urpo Kokko to introduce us and to arrange a time for us to meet. I would not have guessed ahead of time how nice and easy-going WA Back was. I felt at ease in his company.

We headed south from the city along the Brisbane River. After about a 15-minute drive we passed the large buildings of the university in St Lucia, where along the river the wealthy have resided amongst the greenery. We stopped in front of a bright double-storey modern mansion. At the end of the garden path above the door there was a sign written in brass letters that read 'MUNSALA'. It informs the (Finnish) guests of Mr Back's old home region in Finland. We rang the doorbell and a tall middle-aged man answered the door.

'Mr Back is not quite ready, but come in. I am his son-in-law,' he said and directed us to the living room. 'Mr Back was not expecting you for another hour. He is busy at the moment, but let's see if he can see you sooner.'

'Oh gosh, I understood on the phone that this was the time to meet. We don't want to intrude. Perhaps we can come back a little later?' said Urpo.

'Don't worry, have a seat, I have some time now,' we heard Mr Back say from the next room.

A cheery old man who seemed to be in his 60s came in. He was wearing casual work clothes and his shoes were covered in dust and mud. 'It's best to do some work at this age to stay fit,' he said. 'I haven't felt this energetic and fit in a long time. Yesterday I thought I better get some proper work done and I got my shovel out. I have been working hard since morning, perhaps too hard. I'm sorry, I will get myself cleaned up, I won't be a moment.'

He would like a hundred descendants

After talking for a couple of hours we agreed I would come back the next day with cameras. When I returned he had a nice tie and a pressed shirt on. Despite this he was still the same energetic and carefree old man as I had met yesterday.

'I have the whole day free and I'm also available tomorrow. We can do whatever you like. Just let me know and I will organise it,' he laughed. 'I think I've earned some time off by now whenever I want. In fact, I'm retired.'

Mr Back came to Australia 61 years ago at the age of 17. It was hard to believe that he was already 78 years old. He will probably always be young at heart. I spent the whole day with him and the time flew by. We enjoyed lunch at a restaurant on top of Mt Coot-tha. You could see the whole city from up there. You could also see the university in St Lucia and the areas that he had purchased years ago just as forests, which he had then developed.

'They say that you are Australia's richest Finn?'

'I am not rich. At least I don't consider myself that way. It's a different story with those who give large donations...'

'But at least from native Finns.'

'Well, I suppose I have had success in my work. However, I am retired now. I have divided my farms to my children and my grandchildren. I have four boys and a girl, and 24 grandchildren from which of those five are already married. They also have five children. I hope to live to see the day that I have 70 grandchildren, which would make 100 descendants.'

Later I heard that Mr Back had actually given some donations himself. It's been said that after the war he gifted 10,000 sheep to children in Europe; however I didn't get to confirm this with him personally.

Mr WA Back is mainly known as a sheep farmer. However, he has also operated as a builder and he owns many properties around Brisbane. He is also a shareholder in the world's largest copper mine located in Mount Isa.

'I actually have Governor-General Bobrikov to thank for all of this, since we fled (Finland) with my father in 1902 to escape from Bobrikov's conscription laws, my father was considering where to flee. He said, 'There are too many negroes in America, Canada is too cold, there are too many problems in Africa, New Zealand has earthquakes and it might sink into the sea...' and then finally we were left with Australia. His original plan was to bring his whole family over, however he realised that Australia was too primitive. He didn't want to be a frontiersman and after two weeks he decided to return back to Finland. He left me £400 that he had brought with him for initial capital.

'My brother had been here already two years and so we came to stay with him. I still remember the welcome greeting when we first arrived in Australia. It was a late night when we arrived at my brother's farm and he asked if we wanted some eggs for dinner. When we went to fetch the eggs we found a 5-metre snake eating a chicken.'

Wool trade saved me from bankruptcy

Mr WA Back stayed and worked on his brother's farm, which was located around a couple of hundred kilometres south of Brisbane in Cape Byron. For 12 months he worked to clear the land and managed 22 Indians whom his brother had hired. He learnt to speak Hindi. After that he bought 230 hectares of land, which cost two pounds per hectare. These days the value is 30 times that as in 450 marks per hectare.

Young William's farm was merely 'bush'. The closest road was 5 kilometres away and the closest residential area was 15 kilometres away.

'My father wrote that if you want to succeed there you will need to find a good family and get married. If you find a Finnish wife, she will always long to return back home and you won't feel settled to stay (in Australia). So that is what I did and I found a lovely lady, Christina Hart, who was a year younger than me. Her family originally came from England, however she was born here. We got married in 1907, however before then she bought 300 hectares of land under her name. According to the regulations she would not have been able to do this as a married woman, since a family or a single person could not own two separate land areas. You couldn't buy land as an investment, but you had to live on the land for the purpose of clearing it otherwise you would lose rights to own it. So it seemed that we had to live separately on our own land. Of course this would have been impossible. So we took a risk and thought beforehand which piece of land we would give up if it came to it. Then we found a loophole which allowed us to live together as long as the distance between the farmlands was within 50 kilometres. The distance was actually 100 kilometres, however when we had the officials look into it, on the map the distance over the mountain between the properties was

50 kilometres. As a result, we were able to start clearing the land for a banana plantation (keeping both properties).

'In all honesty, if I knew where Bobrikov was buried I would take flowers to his grave (to thank him). So many times in my life it has happened where, after a tragedy, good fortune has followed. When everything seems to be going wrong, I have been able to find a solution from elsewhere.

'In fact, that is how I came to have sheep, which has turned out to be the best thing. In 1914 my health could not withstand the humid climate on the coast, as a result I got bad bronchitis so we had to move west to a drier climate... just where the sheep lands were. I had a good credit rating and so I was able to get a loan from the bank. That is how I was able to get started and the sheep multiplied 108 percent in the first year. These days you would have to have about 10 000 pounds or 70 000 marks before you could start sheep herding and make a living.

'In 1950 once again I had to flee and leave everything behind. At that time, I had 50 houses being built at the same time in this area in St. Lucia. However, after the war the regulations and material requirements changed which meant that nothing was going my way. I had a nervous breakdown and the doctor recommended that I take a holiday somewhere. I left all of the projects behind and my wife and I departed for Finland via America. I did bring my wool samples with me which I had not been able to sell. When we arrived in America the Korean War started and America needed wool in a hurry for the army. I immediately sent a message home for all of the 300 bales to be sent over. That way I was first in line and I was able to sell them all for 180 pounds (1300 marks). The value of the bales back home was only 40 pounds (290 marks).

'When I returned the officials were asking why I was able to continue the building projects. The building sites had been abandoned and untouched for 7 months. Now I did not have any (money) troubles. I was able to get what I needed and so I was able to finish the houses. You have to believe in yourself, young man. You need to believe in what you do. Especially those who are in a creative and important position. Otherwise it will not work,' Mr Back said and smiled.

'The first time I visited Finland with the whole family was in 1923. Erik, my oldest son, was 15 years old. Elwyn was 11, Aubrey was 9, Gloria was 3 and Alan was 2 years old. I bought a car in Italy from Turin and we drove through Europe to Stettin from where we sailed on Ariadne to Helsinki. We spent the whole 3 months of summer in Finland. It was a good summer. Erik was surprised that it was hotter in Finland than back home in Australia. I would love to go back to Finland one more time to go around Saimaa. The pine forests, the long days and the bright nights.' Mr William Andrew Back, the sheep farmer and big businessman sighed and smiled.

'We forget everything tedious in our lives and remember the good and beautiful.'

THE 'BIG HOUSE' LOUNGE ROOM

COME, JOIN ME IN A WALK through the 'Big House.'

My most vivid childhood memories of it centre in the lounge room. There, two statues fascinated and inspired me. One depicted a girl threading a needle. Chosen perhaps, because Grandma Christina was expert at dressmaking and mending, adjusting hand-me-down clothes during a battler upbringing. Her husband would enable her dream to buy ornate new dresses in the capital cities of the world.

My favourite statue was the barefoot boy cradling his dead bird in gentle hands, shoulders slumped with grief. A cousin emailed me a photo of it and again I marvel that the translucent tear on his cheek is stone. Why did you choose this expression of grief, Grandad? Did it strike a chord, propel you back to the young lad who grieved over deaths of brothers, a sister back in Finland?

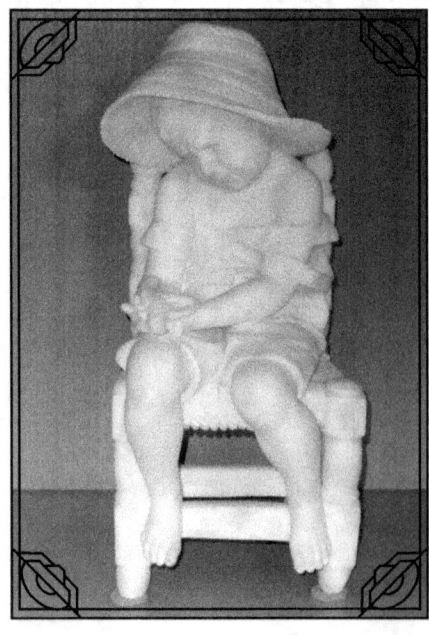

FURTHER BACK

DECADES LATER, MY FINNISH FAMILY shared early family photographs and I marvel at the resemblances. My great-grandfather's chin, that Swedish fair complexion that reappears in grandchildren. The heritage that has been preserved in precious photographs, so we can see the people from whom we came. As my father's cousin Wally Holm would say: 'Now we must take a photograph.'

Auspicious occasions warrant a family photograph. So this may celebrate the first communion of eldest surviving son, Karl Johan Back (born 20 October, 1877) on 24 June, 1894. If so, the child on my great-grandmother Sanna Back's lap was Edvard, born 10 January 1895, and died 17 October 1933.

Or this first family photograph might be dated 1892, the dark year when two children died a month apart; little Johanna on the 21st of February, aged ten months. Anders had called her his little Easter lily-of-the-valley, for she was born on Easter Saturday. Her name meant *'God is gracious'* — a bitter irony.

Her three-year old brother, Nils Edvard, followed just a month later on March 20.

But let us take the former option.

My grandfather's expression reveals one who has shared grief from his formative age. Grandma also grew up shadowed by two sisters, Fanny Elizabeth and Elsie May, who both died in infancy before her own birth. We can imagine why, amid the many others on offer, the poignant grief of this sculpture resonated with both grandparents.

Grandad bought these two statues in Italy in 1924, on a year-long Grand Tour to Finland to introduce his wife and children to his parents, sister and brother. WA Back sailed from Sydney on 15 February 1924 on the *SS Osterly*, together with an entourage of wife Christina, five children and a nurse.

They disembarked in Toulon, France, on the Mediterranean coast, then took a train to Turin in Italy. Grandad's postcard from Ventimiglia on the Italian Riviera already rued this travelling circus:

> It's so boring to travel with so many to look after, especially with so many children, and fifteen bags. We should have come straight from England so we wouldn't have everything with us.

Shopping expeditions in Paris, Zurich and London added more luggage.

Eric, the eldest son, noted in his diary:

> Father got a craze on Genoese Sculptury [sic] and ended up with a large consignment to Australia.

The shipment included Venetian glassware, which would be displayed in a glass cabinet, but never used for fear the gold trim would wash off. It was topped by a large ornate china fruit bowl for a grand table setting. Other ceramics were stored under the stairs.

> At the Fiat factory, Dad ordered a large six-cylinder car but as it would not be ready for 20 days we took a leisurely tour of northern Italy; Venice, Florence, Genoa and Milan. We had ample time to see thousands of paintings.

Fifty years later, my husband Antoni and I also made a less Grand Tour to Europe with three sons and a school orchestra. The latter flew home and we roamed in a campervan for three months through the winter, visiting 16 countries as friends were scattered around the continent. We celebrated Christmas in a *gasthaus* at Oberammergau. There, my eye and heart were drawn to a wooden carving of a child nestled into a hand. Never mind the tight budget, my spirit yearned to buy this. It stood on my dressing table until last year when I passed it on to a son as a tribute to his own nurturing spirit.

The 'Big House' sculptures inspired me, my siblings and cousins to artistic creations. During my teens clay was most accessible. Later, a friend helped me to cast into metal my attempt to depict the Debussy *Rhapsody* that I learned and performed while studying at the University of Queensland. What to do with it when I moved out? With no place to store it, I deposited it into bushes behind Grace College. Imagine the puzzled faces when workmen bulldozed it up during developments.

–You raised cultured children, Grandad, giving them the opportunities to visit art galleries.

–Yes, we gave our family an awareness of the good things in life, of music and art, of our heritage. Faith.

–We were cash-strapped for a decade after our European tour. How did you afford it?

–As we planned to visit Mother and Father in Finland I foolishly invested in Mullumbimby land.

```
I jumped ahead of myself, thinking that big
venture would pay for our trip Overseas. I took
note of Boxall, the Town Clerk and picked up his
subdivision of Morrison Park, which looked so
promising and sure. Simultaneously I had gone
into Coronation Park with Offner and others and
I also went in with Ted Hardy for the Ingham
Sugar land, which turned out to be a wasted
effort. The Premier of Queensland cancelled the
building of the sugar mill on the Ingham land
and put it on the much poorer land at Tully...
Likewise Coronation Park was a 25-year delay
and all we used to get were periodical rows and
arguments with Offner & Hadley, but the hand of
God was in it and after all these years now God
has blessed us in this St Lucia venture.
```

–So you planned to sell art works back in Australia?

– One can only try and, if a venture does not succeed, there are other possibilities.

–After your death in 1974, we moved to England where I studied sculpture—I was more interested in that than music. I enrolled for part-time sculpture classes at John Cass Art College in East London. The inimitable Quentin Crisp was a model for life drawing classes.

I even poured the bronze for a little piece and wish I had prepared more of my wax works for casting. After carrying them round the Continent, to Sweden and Germany and France, when we arrived back in Australia they shrivelled away in that first summer's heat.

–Nothing is wasted.

–That's not what you said a page ago, but I caught your gist; keep multi projects simmering away and some will prove edible.

–Grandad, you described yourself as an uneducated man, but my research into your upbringing shows you must have understated. Just six kilometres from your home in Munsala at Storsved was the Svedberg School, renowned as innovative through all of Finland.

–It was the forerunner of Finnish education, respected then as now. Its library was one of the largest among Finland's primary schools.

THE MUNSALA MILIEU OF WA BACK'S UPBRINGING

MUNSALA WAS A CULTURED HUB of intellectuals: Judge Hällsten and his petite wife Betty hosted soirées for cultural leaders like educational innovator and journalist Anders Svedberg; Jonas Castrén, professor of literature; poet Arvid Mörne; Zacharias Topelius from nearby Nykarleby. Johan Ludvig Runeberg, Finland's national poet, was born in neighbouring Jakobstad.

It was inevitable that such luminaries opposed Russian Oppression.

The Tsar signed decrees that Bobrikov should shut down newspapers and that printing presses must obtain a Board of

Censors permit to print papers. Soon, Bobrikov took control of censorship by establishing an Advisory Committee on Press Affairs. Thus the Board of Censors was relegated to the status of a mere post office. The manifesto forbad 'needless consideration of the conscription issue in newspapers' and inappropriate criticism or headlines hostile to Russia.

A photograph shared by my Finnish family may commemorate Grandad's first communion, taken before he and Anders left Finland. On the back Wally Holm has pencilled the ages; sisters Anna Sanna 19 and Sofia 14; Edvard 2. (He was born in 1895 so would be perhaps four years old if this were taken in 1900.) Wilhelm is 14; maybe this was taken shortly before his 15th birthday. Anders Back's sister sits on the right.

The boy who stood tall for his family photo, his arm resting against his father's right shoulder, surely knew that this was the important memento to sustain his mother — and father — through the coming years of loneliness, when they'd be missing two sons.

His father Anders looks up to the camera with an enigmatic acceptance but the mouth is clamped into determination. 'Trust me, son,' he seems to say, 'it will be for your own good; you can make a safe future, a rich future with this new start. I will teach you all the skills I can to see you ahead, will take you across in safety. After that you make your own fortune in life.'

Sporting an uneven basin haircut, Wilhelm's lips part in anticipation — he's eager to take the challenge.

Anders Back shepherded Wilhelm and three other lads from Munsala by train to the southern port, Hanko (Hangö in Swedish). They sailed on *SS Arcturus* for England, where they embarked on *SS Ophir*.

ARRIVAL IN SYDNEY, JANUARY 1903

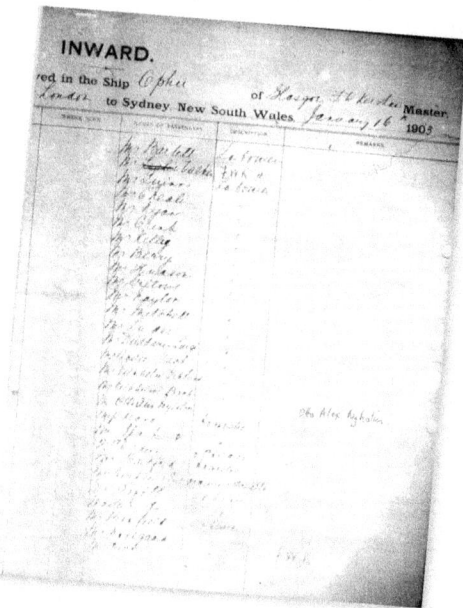

Shipping records prove the voyagers arrived in Sydney Harbour on 17 January 1903. Soon after, they boarded a train to Lismore and Bangalow. There, brother Karl Johan Back welcomed them and took them to his rough 'house' in a black butt tree.

Or was it 1902, as WA Back's niece Alice Holm wrote in her memoir?

> On the 17th January 1902 Grandfather Anders together with fifteen-and-a half year old Wilhelm (later known as William or Will) alighted from the train at Bangalow.

In my recorded interview with Grandad's nephew Wally Holm he states that they had to leave before WA turned 16 as the Russian officials prohibited travel from that age. Yet as WA arrived in Australia in January 1903, that would make him aged 16.5, turning 17 at the end of July, for his birth was 1886.

Emigrating in November 1902, he was past his 16th birthday and there may have been concern that the Russian authorities would prevent their leaving. Indeed, WA himself added confusion by stating on his naturalisation certificate his arrival as January 1902 rather than 1903. Surely he could not mistake the date of such a significant life change? Often in this family, numbers don't add up. WA and his brother KJ tended to fudge dates by a year, perhaps to cover their traces in case they were tracked to the other end of the globe. For, as we often heard, 'Russians have long memories.'

But leave WA did, settle and make good he did. He took his father's advice and married a fine Australian wife who made a fitting helpmate for over 60 years.

Wally Back told me in his lilting Swedish accent: 'Well, of course, Wilhelm came out with his father as a boy of sixteen and Anders, he was only in Australia two weeks. Then he went back to Finland but in those two weeks, he bought a farm each for Wilhelm, for KJ and for Edvard, the brother who never made it to the Promised Land.'

Anders said to his sons, 'Settle down here, marry a good Australian girl and forget Finland. This is your land now.'

Back home in Munsala, he repeated his words to wife Sanna. She laughed: 'How can Wilhelm find a wife, who would marry him when he doesn't speak any English?'

'Oh yes, he will find a wife no trouble,' replied Anders. 'What other 16-year old boy has his own farm already at this age?'

MARRIAGE 1908

Grandad heeded his father's advice and married Christina Hart.

In a personal letter dated 28 February 1974, a few weeks before my own wedding on 16 March 1974, he reflected on this marriage. He also offered advice for our future, and mentioned that the wet climate around Byron Bay area triggered bronchitis. (This would lead his paths north of the border to Queensland.)

> As I look back now on our marriage at Mooball on the 4th November, 1908, I can remember it as plain as if it was yesterday. We only had one visitor with us, a Percy Smith from Sydney, who was working for me on the farm, but there was my brother KJ and the Hart family. Yes, the wedding was in our new home, which I had finished only a few days before the wedding, and the minister from Byron Bay came by train to perform the wedding. We had a very nice wedding breakfast—

– I can imagine, knowing the Hart hospitality! I remember as a child visiting Aunty Inez (Christina's sister-in-law) and my eyes popping to see a table laden with cakes, scones and biscuits. She must have baked all day before we arrived.

—Indeed. But you interrupt me.

> And as the southward train was leaving at 4 o'clock everybody was off the place and we just sat down and looked around.

St. Lucia Presbyterian Church

DEDICATION of PIPE ORGAN

THE GIFT OF
Mr. and Mrs. W. A. BACK

SUNDAY, 13th JUNE, 1954
At 11 a.m.

PARTICULARS OF THE INSTRUMENT

Organ built by Messrs. Whitehouse Bros., Brisbane.

The organ consists of two manuals of 61 notes, CC to C and a pedal keyboard of 30 notes CCC to F.

The action throughout is tubular pneumatic, wind being supplied to one reservoir by an electric rotary blower.

SPECIFICATION OF STOPS

GREAT ORGAN—
1. Open Diapason — 8 feet metal—61 pipes.
2. Principal — 4 feet metal—61 pipes.
3. Dulciana — 8 feet metal—61 pipes.

SWELL ORGAN (Enclosed)—
4. Oboe — 8 feet metal—61 pipes.
5. Salicional — 8 feet metal—61 pipes.
6. Lieblich Gedact — 8 feet metal—61 pipes.

PEDAL ORGAN—
7. Bourdon — 16 feet wood—30 pipes.

COUPLERS—
8. Swell Super
9. Swell to Great
10. Swell to Great Super
11. Swell to Pedal
12. Great to Pedal

ACCESSORIES—
13. Tremulant (on Swell Organ).
    Balanced Swell Pedal.
    Organ Blower.

There are 396 pipes in the organ, ranging in speaking length from 8 feet to 1/4 of an inch.

ORDER OF SERVICE
SUNDAY, 13th JUNE, 1954
11 a.m.

Doxology (Unaccompanied)
Dedication of Organ—
   Scripture Sentences.
   Presentation of Organ by Mr. and Mrs. W. A. Back.
   Acceptance by Minister for the Congregation.
   Dedication.
Te Deum Laudamus—(Hymn 718).
Prayer of Thanksgiving and Petition.
Scripture Reading.
Psalm 23—"The Lord's My Shepherd."
Scripture Reading.
Solo—Mrs. E. V. Nelson
Prayer and Lord's Prayer.
Offering and Dedicatory Prayer.
Intimations.
Anthem—"I Will Feed My Flock" (Caleb Simper).
Children's Sermon.
Hymn 177—"Come, Children, Join To Sing."
   (Children Retire.)
Sermon.
Prayer.
Hymn 7—"Glory Be To God The Father."
Benediction.
Amen (Sung).

Minister: REV. R. H. C. CROWE.
Guest Organist: MR. JOHN BROUGHTON.

MR. AND MRS. W. A. BACK

WHEN the Presbyterians of St. Lucia witnessed the laying of the Foundation Stone of the new Church, one of the first, and one of the most heartening promises, was that of Mr. and Mrs. W. A. Back who undertook to be responsible for the cost of a suitable pipe organ. A small Committee was appointed to make the necessary enquiries and to decide what would best fulfil the requirements of our Church and the very fine instrument, which is being dedicated to-day to the glory of God and to His service is the happy achievement. The organ is an example of one of the most noble of all musical instruments, still unsurpassed in beauty of natural tone and will add much, musically, to our worship.

To the generous donors who are both loyal and active members of our Congregation, is extended the sincere appreciation of the Minister, Kirk Session, Committee of Management and the Congregation.

RECITALS

Three of Brisbane's leading Organists, assisted by soloists, will be providing recitals as shown below:—

Sunday, 13th June, at 3 p.m.—MR. ARCHIE DAY.

Friday, 25th June, at 8 p.m.—MR. NOEL CLARK.

Sunday, 4th July, at 3 p.m.—MR. HUGH BRANDON.

There will be no admission charge to any of these recitals, but a collection will be taken to help defray the cost of the installation of the organ.

— PLEASE COME AND BRING YOUR FRIENDS —

A GIFT OF MUSIC

Grandad continued in his letter that he amazed his bride with a gift:

> It was certainly a great surprise to Christina, as I had not told her that I had bought a Lipp Piano which was installed in the drawing room and this was such a surprise to the Hart family and even Uncle KJ (my brother).

–I've heard the Harts were musical. That solves something in my mind; I wondered if I was a cuckoo-in-the-nest to become a musician amongst graziers.

–*I was proud to hear you won a competition.*

–If only you'd told me! I craved affirmation, encouragement. You wrote to my faither: *'An idealist cannot succeed. An idealist cannot be happy in life.'* I understood you only valued business. My sap of creativity dried like parched waterholes.

–*You inherited musical talent from the Hart side. I sponsored my niece Perry to study violin in Holland. She was a world-class performer.*

–Wish you'd sponsored me also! But when we were poor students in London, she became our mother figure; gave us meals, home-baked bread and tips to pick nettles from the Thames tow-path and cook them into nutritious soup. I still have her recipes.

–*Let me continue. Christina was very much taken with the piano and she received it with the greatest admiration and wanted somebody to teach her. So after the visitors had gone, we rang up a Piano Teacher from Mullumbimby and she was most delighted to become Christina's teacher.*

–I don't remember hearing Grandma play. But then I have too few memories of her. Cousin Jenny told me she won a book in a school singing competition. And that the Hart and Back family sang around the piano in the Mullumbimby days.

> Then we knelt at the bedside and asked God to protect and guide and bless us through our lives. And we certainly asked for some material blessings that in the eyes of the Lord were very small and he blessed us with very much more than ever we contemplated or asked for. If you take God into your partnership I am sure it will be even better than what you anticipate.

Grandma's duty letters to Finland mention that the boys all learned piano. A cousin remembers practising on a piano in the lounge.

Thank you Grandad for writing your personal letter to me before my own wedding.

WA Back later gifted £2000 for an organ to his parish church, opposite Ironside State School where I endured Grades 1 and 2.

Once a week the 'Proddy' sheep—Protestants—are separated from 'Cattle ticks'—Catholics—and fielded off to Religious Instruction. In single file we march across Swann Road to the red brick Presbyterian Church. We fidget through a sermon and sing 'Jesus Wants Me for a Sunbeam' stirred on by swelling tones of the organ.

In those days I don't notice that a plaque on the organ proclaims it as 'The gift of Mr. and Mrs. W. A. Back'. Or that Whitehouse Brothers built it at a cost of £2,365. It was dedicated at the morning service on 13 June 1954 after which the Brisbane City Organist, Archie Day, gave a recital. As in Mullumbimby, Grandad was an elder of the church, which was built in 1952.

The Order of Service noted:

> When the Presbyterians of St Lucia witnessed the laying of the Foundation Stone of the new Church, one of the first, and one of the most heartening promises, was that of Mr. and Mrs. W. A. Back who undertook to be responsible for the cost of a suitable pipe organ. A small Committee was appointed to make the necessary enquiries and to decide what would best fulfil the requirements of our Church and this very fine instrument, which is being dedicated today to the glory of God and to His service is the very happy achievement. The organ is an example of one of the most noble of all instruments, still unsurpassed in beauty of natural tone and will add much, musically, to our worship.
>
> To the generous donors who are both loyal and active members of our Congregation, is extended the sincere appreciation of the minister, Kirk Session, Committee of Management and the Congregation.

After the Doxology and Dedication, the programme proceeded with *Te Deum Laudamus*, Psalm 23, an anthem *I Will Feed My Flock*, and concluded with the hymn *Glory Be To God the Father*.

Where better to launch the second book of my trilogy, *Midnight Sun to Southern Cross*, than this church so significant to our family?

THE MOOBALL HOME

–So, Grandad, as you were born 29th July 1886, you were 22 years old when you married—similar to myself.

–1908 was a big year for me; I became naturalised in February, so I knew my future lay with Australia. There was no prospect of returning to Finland, much as I thought of my family daily. I laboured hard before the wedding, for KJ and I were building a large sawmill on the land at Devil's Lookout, surrounded by forests of splendid hardwood, of cedar trees with rich red timber. As I built the first house to be ready for my bride I dreamed that later I would use that timber in my home.

–Which you did, at Cedar House, a stylish, comfortable home. It sold recently. If only we had a few spare million dollars…

–I worked my fingers to blisters to fell trees, clear the scrub and establish a farm. I built a white fence around it and of course fencing to hold the cows and horses, milking sheds, barns and a dairyman's cottage. Perhaps some jealous peoples said I had an easy start from my Father but he also passed on his work ethic.

I imagine Grandma adds: 'We called it *Rosedale*, for always I loved flowers.'

–You chose well, building near the new train line that opened in 1894.

–It passed by the bottom of our hill, with a station at either side of the farm, at both Mooball and at Burringbar. Cream and milk could be transported direct to the cities, without having to haul it on lorries like many farmers did.

—As the Hart family did up in the ridges of Wilson's Creek.

—*So I was building, building, using skills learned from my father in Munsala at the carpentering bench. Building latticed verandas to catch the breezes, high on a hill. The worst Australian heat shrivelled my body, so I situated homes high to invite the sea breezes. I was so busy that it helped to have the faster travel between Mooball and Wilson's Creek in my little Ford car.*

—I heard that locals feared the new-fangled car. Did they think it would scare the horses?

—*There are always peoples who fight against progress, will laugh behind their hands and point fingers. They feel jealous of us who choose to move with new times.*

In a photograph posed on the verandah, Wilhelm sits back with a satisfied air, china teacup in hand. He smiles benign pride at cherubic baby Elwyn propped in a cane wicker chair. Born 20 November 1912, this must date the photograph 1913. At his right hand Eric rides his hobbyhorse. His knowing gravitas shows he understands how the family back home treasure photographs. That love of visual memory was passed on to me.

The domestic scene of a young emigrant, his modish wife and two children, a maid pouring tea. I feel encouraged; living with Grandad must have been cyclonic, yet my grandparents held together through the years. They set a fine example.

After clearing his Mooball land, WA realized that property development might make a better living than milking cows. Always on the road, he led a busy life while Christina raised five children.

For decades, he commuted between his Mullumbimby base and St Lucia as well as on to pastoral properties in Western Queensland.

His brother Karl Johan Back summed up the dilemma to the folks back in Finland:

> Wilhelm has trouble with his land spread far apart; it would be as if you had your land in Munsala, Nykarleby, Denmark, Sweden, Gibraltar and Palestine.

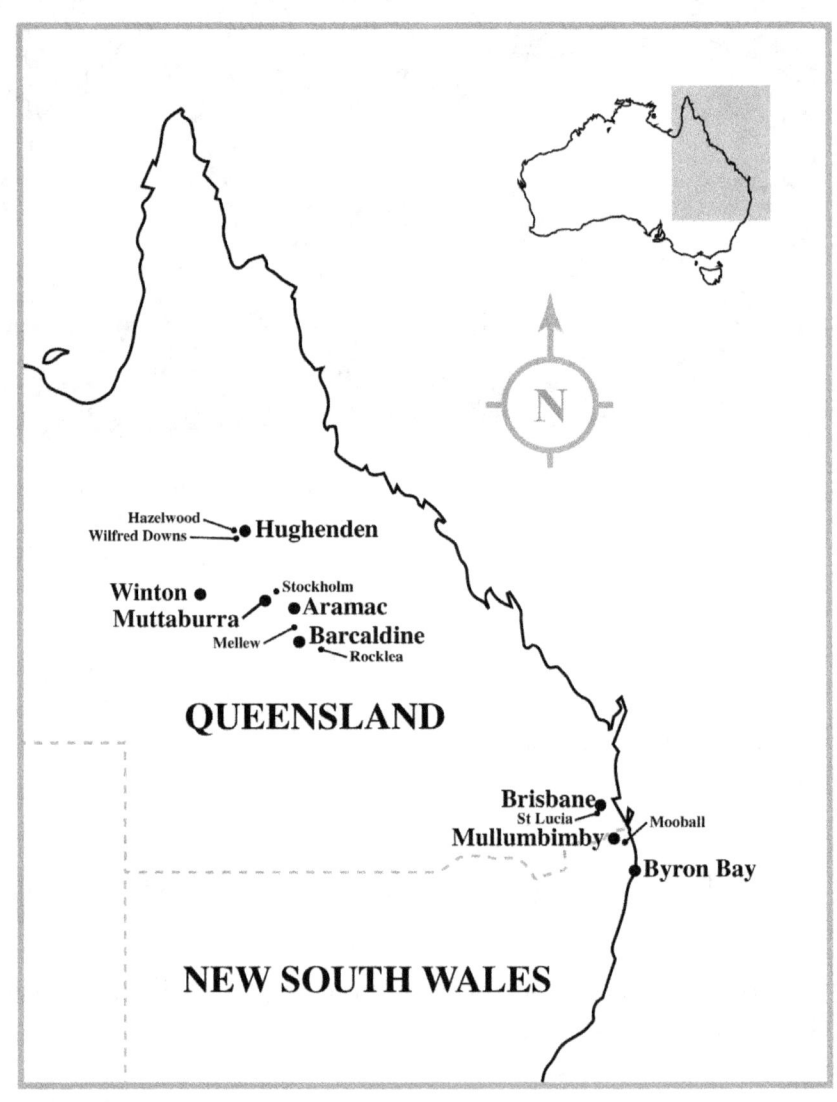

THE SHEEP'S BACK

Further insights into Grandad's move north can be gleaned from his 1974 letter to me:

> While we were living at Mooball up until 1913 or 14 I became very interested in sheep raising and wool growing and at first I thought we would start with sheep on the 320-acre farm between Mooball and Burringbar.

He sought advice in Sydney from Pitt Son and Badgery, where the latter, 'a very old man...condemned the idea of trying to grow wool on the north coast of NSW.' Mr. Badgery took him into the Queensland room, and unrolled a big map on the wall.

> With a pointing stick he picked out Blackall, Barcaldine, Longreach, Winton, Hughenden, Muttaburra, Aramac, and he said this is the place for a young man to go. He could place me in touch with a young fellow that was visiting his parents in NSW. This man had drawn a selection between Winton and Hughenden. He showed his return what he had made for the three years in occupation. 'This is more than what all his family had made in the Riverina in New South Wales, which is classed as the best country for wool growing.' All this was very interesting to me, but I had my place at Mooball Burringbar. I proceeded on to get a dairy herd established there after 150 acres of it was felled and grassed, but neither of us learned to milk, so we had a family run dairy while I devoted my time to clearing the land.

We were settled in there at Mullumbimby, a nice home, a little office. Business life appealed to me very much and certainly it taught me a good deal about financing and banks, and other institutions consulted me. It was a continuous work, night and day. Sometimes I would get a telephone call from Casino or Murwillumbah, and even from Grafton at 10 and 11 o'clock. I would have to go out early in the morning.

It never dawned on me that I would ever think about sheep again, but Dr. Kellas visited next as he was going to Brunswick Heads for a holiday and he popped in to see me. After testing me he said, 'You will never get rid of this unless you go out West.'

I remembered Mr. Badgery's advice of Western Queensland, and I said what about Longreach or Winton? After looking on the map Dr. Kellas felt sure that that climate would be most suitable for me and I could count on being free from catarrh and hay fever while I was there.

> After I pulled myself together and had the place sold at Mooball I took the train to Barcaldine and Longreach. As soon as I got off the train and walked up the street all ailments of hay fever had left me, so now you can see why I came to become so much associated with Western Queensland. It was the dry climate which suited my lungs and ever since that when I had any bad attacks of bronchitis I went out west and it was the best cure.

The Mullumbimby Star tracked Grandad's reconnaissance of other states.

8 February 1912:	W. Back of Mooball touring Qld, NSW, Vic and SA.
18 April 1912:	Mr. Back, one of our most progressive farmers at Burringbar, who has invested in Queensland properties... just returned from Kingaroy.

During these tours, the prospects of St Lucia came to his notice.

KNOW ALL MEN BY THESE PRESENTS that JAMES O'NIEL MAYNE of Auchenflower, Brisbane, in the State of Queensland, Medical Practitioner, his heirs, executors, administrators and assigns is hereby firmly bound UNTO BRISBANE CITY COUNCIL of Brisbane, a body corporate created by and under "The City of Brisbane Act of 1924",(hereinafter referred to as "the Council") to the payment of -

(a) Five thousand pounds (£5,000), or
(b) A sum equal to the amount which may be agreed upon between the Council and the Owners of the lands situate in the county of Stanley, parish of Indooroopilly, and being Subdivisions 143 to 179 inclusive, and Subdivisions 220 to 246 inclusive, of Portions 18, 19 and 20, containing an area of 8 acres 2 roods 12.7 perches, more or less, or determined by the Court as the compensation payable, on the resumption by the Council of the said lands together with all costs, charges and expenses incurred by the Council or which the Council may be liable to pay in or in relation to or arising out of such resumption, and also all costs, charges and expenses which may be incurred by the Council in the closure of any roads separating the said lands, and also all roads separating the lands mentioned and referred to in a Bond given by the said James O'Niel Mayne to the said Council dated the Eighteenth day of October, 1926.

Payment of such sum or from time to time parts thereof to be made forthwith upon receipt by the said James O'Niel Mayne of a certificate or certificates signed by the Town Clerk or Deputy

become liable to such sum or part of an agreement or a determination the said James O'Niel Mayne of such for which payment or payments well nes O'Niel Mayne binds himself, administrators and assigns firmly by these

AS WITNESS the hand and seal of the said James O'Niel Mayne, and dated the twenty-fourth day of November 1926.

NOW the condition of this obligation is such that if the Council shall not on or before the Eighteenth day of January,1927 have resumed the said lands and made a binding offer, open until the Eighteenth day of October, 1927, to the University of Queensland, to convey the same to the said University without profit to the Council as additional land for the site of the new University THEN and in such case the above Bond and obligation shall be null and void, otherwise the same shall be and remain in full force and virtue.

SIGNED SEALED AND DELIVERED by the said JAMES O'NIEL MAYNE, in the presence of:

James O'Niel Mayne.

EARLY ST LUCIA

BRISBANE'S COLONIAL HISTORY COMMENCED when a short-lived Moreton Bay Penal Settlement was built in the 1820s to house recalcitrant criminals. By the early 1840s it had been closed, and the district surveyed to allow the leasing and sale of land. 'Free Settlement' was offered to the remaining small band of government employees and ex-convicts; immigrants arrived by the boat load, bringing with them all the expectation of self-motivated European free settlers.

Most had sufficient funds to either lease land from the investors who had purchased it at the original government land auctions, or assisted by Land Orders, purchase it outright.

The freeholding of a land area that would become St Lucia, Taringa and Indooroopilly commenced in the mid 1850s and by 1862 all the land comprising today's St Lucia and Long Pocket had been sold. Although somewhat isolated, there formed the nucleus of a coherent local community, ahead of its immediate neighbours.

In the mid 1880s and early 1890s, with the prospect of a quick profit, speculators purchased the farms north of Carmody Road, subdivided them and offered house lots for sale to potential investors and homebuilders. The names for two of these estates endured the marketing hype of the time. Developer and grocer William Alexander Wilson named one *The St Lucia Estate* (after his birthplace in the West Indies), now part of the UQ campus, and *The Ironside Estate* (after his wife's maiden name) bounded by Ryans Road.

Part of St Lucia was known as Lang's Farm, named in honour of the Reverend John Dunmore Lang. After Richard Gailey purchased Lang's Farm, it was subdivided for cane plantations. A 'Proposed New Holiday Resort' was offered to the government, at 'low cost' as a public park called Coronation Park. As early as 1913, the area was suggested as a possible site for the University of Queensland.

Its registrar received a letter from Isles, Love and Co:

7 November 1913

Dear Sir,

We have pleasure in forwarding herewith plan of Coronation Park which you will note has many advantages to commend it as a site for the University.

The block we are offering contains an area of 242 acres 2 roods 4 perches and the price is 100 (one hundred pounds) per acre.

We have also the adjoining block of 130 acres (making 372.5 acres in all) which we are quoting at the same price.

Our clients will be prepared to accept Government Debentures for the land.

If desired, we will arrange to take your Principal out to see the property which can be reached by motor car in ten or twelve minutes.

We think the plan will give you the fullest information with regard to the situation of the land.

Yours faithfully,

The signature is indecipherable.

The University of Queensland began in the 1860s Government House as an interim site, but soon outgrew available teaching space. Residential student accommodation was scattered around the city. Dr James Mayne believed the St Lucia Pocket would be a preferable site for the relocation of the university rather than the Victoria Park option. Together with his sister Mary Emelia, Mayne offered the Brisbane City Council (BCC) £50,000 to purchase the land at St Lucia. They stipulated that BCC had to first offer it to UQ, and if they declined to accept it, then the council was to create a public park.

Historian Andrew Darbyshire muses, in a precis of his 'Land Resumptions – UQ's move to St Lucia', brisbanehistorywordpress.com, April 2020:

> 'Why was broad acre land so close to the city still available? Two reasons initially; it was considered remote, train lines and trams had bypassed it, and only shortly after had it been released onto the market in the mid-1880s there was a series of floods which inundated much of the low lying land. These early 1890s floods, and uncertainty in the banking community, put a dampener on residential development. Even by the 1920s there were only a dozen cottages/houses on the St Lucia Estate and a couple of remaining farmhouses on the land to the south.
>
> 'The gift from the Maynes, increased by two further amounts of £5,000, provided sufficient funds for all the land east of Mill Road (previously Jetty Rd) and part of the 1920s Coronation Park Estate (as far west as Upland Road) to be acquired by BCC. Towards the end of 1926 a Notice of Resumption was placed in the Government Gazette to commence the process, and BCC duly offered the land to the UQ Senate as conditioned by Dr and Miss Mayne.'

Form A.

COMMONWEALTH OF AUSTRALIA

Naturalization Act 1903.

APPLICATION FOR CERTIFICATE OF NATURALIZATION.

TO HIS EXCELLENCY THE GOVERNOR-GENERAL.

Certificate Issued this day.

1. Name in full. 1. I, Wilhelm Anders Back
2. Address and occupation. of Mullumbimby Farmer
hereby apply for a Certificate of Naturalization under the *Naturalization Act* 1903.
3. State "German subject" or "French citizen," &c., as case requires. 2. I am by birth a Swedish native but a Russian Subject
4. Country of previous residence. 3. I arrived in Australia from Hango Finland on the 17th day of January in the year 1902
5. Name of ship. per the Ophir and disembarked at the port of Sydney
6. State places, and periods in each. 4. Since my arrival in Australia I have resided at Mullumbimby and the District surrounding that Town

5. I have resided in Australia continuously for a period of two years immediately preceding the date of this Application.

6. I forward herewith a Statutory Declaration setting forth the particulars required by section 6, sub-section 1, paragraph (α) of the said Act.

7. State whether married or unmarried, and residence of wife. 7. I am unmarried
8. State number. 8. I have no children
9. State number of each sex, and where resident.

9. I am not a naturalized subject or citizen of any other country.
NOTE.—If the Applicant has taken out Naturalization Papers in any other country this statement should be amended accordingly.

10. State the name of the person, and whether he is a Justice of the Peace, Postmaster, Teacher of State School, or Officer of Police. 10. I forward also a certificate signed by William George Norbert Stephens to the effect that I am known to him, and am a person of good repute.

11. Signature of applicant. Wilhelm Anders Back

Dated at Lismore the 5th February 1908.

C.11951.

SET BACK: WORLD WAR I

Letterheads proclaimed Grandad as WA Back.

During the World Wars, anyone with a foreign accent risked internment. So an innocuous surname and abbreviated letters may have saved Grandad and his brother from suspicion. When their sister Anna Sanna joined them in Northern New South Wales in 1920, her husband Erik Johan Nyholm simplified their name to Holm.

WA made great efforts to assert his patriotism by conspicuous donations to the war effort, second only to the mayor's. He raised money by driving people in his new automobile to farewell soldiers—for a fee. Perhaps WA prompted the local newspaper to publish articles to quell the suspicions about him held by the locals. *The Mullumbimby Star* noted on 8 July 1915:

> It has been said that Mr W. Back of this town is of German nationality. On Mr Back's naturalization papers, 18 February, 1908, the place of birth is given as Munsala, Finland, a Swedish part.

On his Application for Naturalisation WA Back answered the question 'I am by birth a...' as 'Swedish native but a Russian subject.' Underlined. His brother Karl Johan described himself as a 'Russian Finn' on his similar Application.

The Mullumbimby Star published a Letter by 'Amen' on 17 June 1915:

> I am simply ashamed of those Australians who so vigorously advocate the internment of all German residents...

5 August 1915:

> W.A. Back the largest individual donor war fund after J.N. Hollingsworth.
>
> W.A. Back of Burringbar donated to Patriotic fund. 5 guineas.

And he also displayed civic duty in World War II:

5 March 1942:

> Mr W.A. Back's offer of use of a garage on the property occupied by Mr H. Duff in Argyle Street as a warden's post, and his permission to dig trenches on a vacant allotment in the same street was accepted with gratitude.

KJ Back's letters home to the Finnish branch of the family showed a need to self-censor:

> There were many things I would have liked to write to you during the war but I feared you would be punished for my sins, so I thought it best to write as little as possible.

Other letters hint that opposing allegiances caused strife between brothers and the more vitriolic ones were burned. The Germans were considered saviours to the Finns, smuggling in weapons on the ship *Equity* to sheltered bays in Ostrobothnia, training the Jäger troops. To Australians, they were enemies; Russians were allies. Brother Edvard fought the 'Reds' in Finland's Civil War. His son Rolf, WA's nephew, during the 1940s Continuation War, took 30 patrols across the border into Russia, wearing camouflage white in winter.

KJ, tending his bananas by lantern light, was suspected of signalling to enemy ships from the hillside. Some muttered he was a spy.

Yet, what is night to a Finn?

SETBACK: SPANISH INFLUENZA

GRANDAD, IN HINDSIGHT, YOU SEEM to have been unstoppable. Always on the go, a power house. So it surprises me to reread your letter of February 1974, that even before the Spanish Influenza hit, you were challenged by health issues.

> At the end of 1913 I became very interested in selling properties all over the north coast, with my little Ford car I was on the road every day, but the district was very wet and I suppose I was careless and I inherited the hay fever every February and March I was laid up with bronchitis. Somebody led me to Dr. Kellas in Lismore and he gave me some good medicine which relieved it from time to time, but every February and March I was completely down to it. It made me feel so tired that I could hardly walk, and Christina often used to say to me 'Shake yourself up, you will be all right.'

–Grandma, I'm pleased to hear you were no doormat to your whirlwind husband! (I can't raise a response from my memories of you.)

–*My loving wife was fading from the effects of dementia when you knew her. It became evident in the 1950s.*

–So that's why I have few personal memories of her.

–*She was a dutiful, loving and caring wife. A helpmate to her husband.*

–I remember her best from photographs, as well-groomed in her pearls, and on special occasions a corsage. I know that she grew up 'hard school' as the eldest surviving daughter of John James Hart (1856–1936) from Whittlesea, Cambridgeshire in England. A week after marrying Harriet Lockings on 19 October 1881, the couple embarked from Plymouth for Australia.

–The Hart family were real battlers, working hard on their farms.

–Grandad, you mention hay fever, and allergies were common after the rainy season. But bronchitis spells lung infection. Did you feel qualms to hear of people dying of 'bronchial weakness' and double pneumonia when Spanish Influenza killed millions in the northern hemisphere in 1918? Knowing it was inevitable that it would spread to Australia, did this escalate your plans to move north of the border? Karl Johan wrote on 24 June 1917 before there was any idea what lay ahead:

```
My brother Wilhelm is now in his home; he is
sick with flu but his family is rather well.
```

Another Mullumbimby missive from KJ on 6 May 1919:

> The Spanish flu is getting closer and closer; it has not yet reached Mullumbimby but we fear it will be here any day. People have already come down with the Spanish flu in Lismore and Bangalow but according to papers no more than 500 have died.

Depleted by World War 1, resources were stretched to cope with the 'Pnu Flu' that hit Europe and then Australia. During the war, reports were suppressed as propaganda.

Antibiotics and penicillin were not available. Treatments included carbolic soap, inoculation and inhalations of zinc sulphate, a noxious chemical that was hoped to neutralise the 'germs' that might lurk in the lungs, throat and mouth. While millions died from Spanish Influenza in the Northern Hemisphere, Australia, an island-protected nation, lost 12,000 citizens, half of them from New South Wales.

When it entered Australia via Sydney in May 1919, government and quarantine officers had already laid contingency plans, with the advantage of foresight and time. A Commonwealth Government planning conference on 26–27 November 1918 involved all states, and produced 13 resolutions. One was that in a case of a state being proclaimed as infected, all human traffic out of that state was to be suspended. The NSW government closed the borders to Victoria after it was accused of failing to implement this measure.

By coincidence, the first media reports about Spanish Influenza and COVID-19 in Australia occurred on 25 January—exactly 101 years apart. Although it was not diagnosed as such, Australia's first case of Spanish flu was admitted to a Melbourne hospital on 9 January 1919.

The NSW government ordered mandatory masks, and closed Sydney libraries, churches, schools, theatres and public entertainment. Comparisons and anomalies abound, as with 2020. Religious worship was forbidden, even outside, social-distanced and masked. Crowds could barrack at football matches, but racecourses were closed.

When Spanish influenza reached the Northern Rivers district, the *Mullumbimby Star* reported on 6 February 1919:

> There is one thing in the country dweller's favour with the epidemic, and that is that fresh air and sunshine are death on the germ. A Melbourne doctor has spoken out on this. He says to wear a mask when in close contact with likely cases, but 'In the name of common sense, breathe in the air pure and unadulterated.' There is no other kind of air but the pure in Mullumbimby, so we should be moderately safe. At the same time all precautions should be taken. While the medical men are fighting the common foe, influenza, the politicians are also having a fight on State Rights! A little trade is being deflected and the insects are buzzing around and threatening reprisals.

It became impossible for the Commonwealth to continue any pretence at controlling traffic when State Governments were not only acting independently, but were every day imposing new restrictions without reference to, or consultation with, the Commonwealth Government... relations between New South Wales and Victoria became very strained... the border blockades soon proved to be farcical... and such ludicrous occasions were recorded as that of a dairy farmer being prohibited from crossing the road, which formed the border at that point, to milk his cows on the other side.

KJ continued on 26 June 1919:

> The Spanish influenza has now covered almost all of Australia and Mullumbimby was the last town in our area but even we have it here now and the doctor was the first and so far the last to have died. He was a heavy drinker and as far as I can understand it is almost impossible for a drinker to overcome that disease. Many die also because they leave bed way too early. I also think that we got a milder form of the disease than other parts of the world. I'm as healthy as ever and so is our brother and his family.

That month, Mayor Joe Hollingworth died of the Spanish flu at the young age of 54. His executors used money from his will to buy KJ's land and sawmill.

–That was a venture in which you were a sleeping partner, Grandad. Did you feel mortality creep closer when Frank James died on 29 September, just 50 years old?

–He was a neighbour and acquaintance, one of the first peoples I met when I arrived in January 1903, one of my best customers.

Near to home, footballer Arthur Henry Soutar, aged 32, died on 28 June 1919, just before the Saturday Burringbar vs. Mullumbimby game. The spectators stood bareheaded in silence as a tribute, and each member of the Burringbar team wore a white band.

On 27 June, the Tweed Daily published an article titled *The Coat Men*.

> The password in the street and on the roads today is: 'Have you had it?'
>
> The reply is generally 'Yes,' with a wan smile that in itself tells the tale of the 'flu. It is easier now to count the population that has not had the 'flu and those who have; convalescents are to be seen everywhere... they mostly have a

big overcoat, which is worn throughout the day.
They don't walk—they just move along with slow and
unmeasured step and as they come closer you perceive
a pale and sickly face. It is the 'flu alright.

You enquire. 'Oh, I only had a mild attack,'
comes the reply, and then 'But it was good
enough for me.' They all start to tell you how
weak they feel; no appetite for work. The only
appetite they have is to wander aimlessly about
or sit down in some snug corner with a big coat
on and in the warm sunshine... There is one
universal aftermath and that is weakness...

But.

There is a warmth about human kindness which
the 'flu has caused hundreds of people in this
district to feel and appreciate as they have
never done in their lives before.

'Have you had it yet?'

No—then you possibly have yet to come into the
pleasant glow of this warmth and comradeship
which is the child of adversity.

Victoria suffered the worst fatality rate; states bickered over closures.

How did people fare across the border in Queensland? Police shut the borders and established quarantine camps along the southern boundary.

Crossings were permitted at Wallangara where those wishing to enter Queensland were required to pay from 7s 6d to 12s 6d a day for the pleasure of seven days' detention, two injections and thrice daily ten-minute stints in an inhalation chamber. Advance bookings were taken by the Tourist Bureau in Sydney. For several weeks living conditions in the camp were abominable and only intercession by the Anglican Archbishop secured separate ladies' toilets.

Travellers were required to quarantine in the camps for seven days before entering the state. In 1919, the main camps were at Wallangarra and Coolangatta.

Attempts to control infection included inspection of all ships entering Queensland, isolation of population, closure of places of public assemblage such as theatres and churches, and inoculation. Hospitals overflowed and 400 temporary beds were set up in huts at the Brisbane Exhibition Grounds. St Laurence's Christian Brothers School in South Brisbane catered for the overflow from the nearby Mater Hospital temporary accommodation. In 1918–9 there were 9570 cases reported in Brisbane and 11,099 elsewhere in Queensland. Unlike previous outbreaks of influenza, many of the 830 deaths from the disease in Queensland in 1919 were young adults; 69 deaths among the 596 residents of the Barambah aboriginal settlement.

Having discussed with medical practitioners, including Dr Phillip Cumpston, the grandson of the Director of Quarantine (1913–1945), John Howard Lidgett Cumpston, I acknowledge it might be a stretch to wonder if Grandad was over-concerned by bacterial pneumonia and respiratory tracts. The viral vs. bacterial question is beyond this novice. Yet, this appears to be another factor that prompted my grandfather to stretch his wings and move from Mullumbimby north of the state border into Queensland—and thus eventually to St. Lucia.

DELIVERANCE

Providence intervened when a bequest by Dr and Miss Mayne enabled the University of Queensland to proceed in St Lucia. The Brisbane City Council resumed 200 blocks between 1926 and 1929 for the site of the University.

A meeting between James Mayne and Brisbane City Council relating to the resumption of land at St Lucia notes:

> At 3.15pm on Tuesday the 19th October 1926 the Aldermen of the Brisbane City Council resumed their adjourned Council Meeting at St Lucia. In the company of Dr. James Mayne, they inspected the land Council proposed to resume as a possible site for the University of Queensland. The previous day on the 18th October James had signed a bond with the Brisbane City Council agreeing to fund the cost of land resumption for the site. If the University chose not to accept the site, it was planned that the land would become a public park, furthering Jolly's vision of a green belt for the City of Brisbane. James Mayne entered into an original agreement with Brisbane City Council to provide funds for land acquisition on the 18th October 1926. This was then revised and signed on 24th December 1926 when the true cost of acquisition of the site became apparent. At the time James entered into the original agreement it was uncertain whether the land would be used for a University or Public Park. According to the original deed the University had until 18th of October 1927 to accept the gift of land as a new site for the University. In reality, it was to be May 1930 before the University officially accepted the land.

The Government and University of Queensland dithered whether to accept this offer. Meanwhile, in 1933–38, the St Lucia land was used for the state-funded Farm School, where hundreds of city boys were trained to plough, sow crops and milk cows.

RESUMPTION OF LAND

Brisbane City Council negotiated with many St Lucia residents to resume their land; both Coronation Park estate properties and also the St Lucia Estate. Local Historian Andrew Darbyshire has documented this process (brisbanehistorywordpress.com, April 2020):

> 'The individual land owners were required to make a claim for compensation which was considered initially by the City Valuer. Then began the serious business of negotiation, and the correspondence files make for some interesting reading. No one seems to have received what they thought reasonable, although there is a thread that they recognised that the resumption was for a worthy cause… It is evident from the settlements that there was a marked difference in land value. The lots in the old St Lucia Estate were valued at around £30 on average (£50–60 riverside), on the more recently released Coronation Park Estate £70–110. The 'backbone' of the latter was Coronation Drive, today's Hawken Drive, and its planning and layout were lauded at its launch. It was considered a significant step forward by the newly reinvigorated Town Planning Association of Queensland. Allotments were 20 perches (rather than the more normal 16) and streets laid out to follow the contours of the land.

> 'The standard Coronation Park Conditions of Sale are informative. They included clauses that prevented the erection of duplicate house designs on adjacent lots, prevented the building of business premises other than in the nominated zones, and limited trade activity on any lot without agreement

by at least 75% of the owners in the same section. The type of development control that wouldn't be introduced by government for decades.'

The Brisbane City Council file contains many letters to the effect that:

> We are acting for the purchaser of the above property, and on his behalf we make claim for compensation in respect for the resumption for the sum of ₤282.

Below a comment in red ink notes 'Offer of £200 recommended; (and handwritten) 'without prejudice.'

Further letters bemoaned:

> ... Unexplained delay in dealing with the resumption on behalf of our clients... We received 32 letters on behalf of various clients dated 4 March 1927, making an offer for full settlement of the claim... We are daily receiving letters from our clients asking when the matter is to be fixed up.

The Council replied:

> Having submitted claims and having promptly received offers, do you not think, unless you intend to adhere to the amounts of your original claims, although you have not stated so in any of your letters, that the next step lies with you? The Council is at all times willing to try and arrange amicable settlements, but the amounts claimed in the instances under discussion preclude that course being followed.

WA Back wrote to The Town Clerk, City Council Chambers, Brisbane.

13th September 1927

Dear Sir,

Re-Coronation Park Resumptions

Referring to your notification of 17th February of the above resumptions, my boys have been anxiously expecting a settlement as Messrs. Offner, Hadley & Co., advised me last month that your Council were ready to settle

I will therefore deem it a great favour if you could expedite matters and remit the cheques. They are only small sums, but it will gladden young hearts to receive their money.

Yours faithfully,

W. A. Back

And on 29 September 1927:

> I, William Andrew Back, of Mullumbimby, in the state of New South Wales, grazier, do hereby solemnly and sincerely declare as follows:
>
> On the fth day of March, 1924, I entered into an agreement for sale with Coronation Park Limited for the purchase of the land described as Lots 51, 52, 53, of portion 18, County of Stanley, parish of Indooroopilly. In this Agreement for Sale, it is set forth that the property was sold to me as guardian for Eric William John Back, who is my son and a minor. (Aged 17 years at the present time.)

Land was held in the names of Eric, Aubrey, and Alan Back. There was no mention of middle son Elwyn.

Through the resumption process Coronation Park had to keep a close eye on their books, the resumptions included not only unsold land, but also blocks sold on 'terms' over a period of years.

The National Bank was also involved when loans had been raised and/or purchasers were in default (the National Bank of Australia had 'inherited' the land through its predecessors —likely due to mortgage default originally). They appear to have relied on the Coronation Park account keepers to keep them up to date. No houses had been built on the land resumed in this estate.

The Brisbane City Council files divulge argy-bargy haggling over resumption valuations. Handwritten letters reveal the angst of the women caught up in the slipstream.

One wrote on 27 September 1927:

> The City Council Valuer has offered me ₤350 which is impossible for me to accept, for it would not buy one another home of any kind whatsoever. My husband is an Invalid Inmate at Dunwich and I have to depend solely on my two sons one at present out of employment, my Income being ₤2.5.0 a week. I cannot afford to pay rent or Instalments. All I am asking of the Council is ₤400... and my Property is Absolutely Worth it.

Another on 10 November, 1927:

> Dear Sir,
>
> I at no time agreed with either Mr Wightman or anyone else to accept ₤350, and hold Mr Wightman's letter to corroborate this. But apart from this altogether, if the Council compulsorily deprive me of my land and home, then it is only right for them to compensate me to the full value of same and not on the other hand endeavour to beat me below that. My price is ₤400 and I am not prepared to take less.
>
> Yours faithfully,
>
> Mrs Smedley

Timing was too tight for 'Harry' Angel the 'radio ham', Mr and Mrs Henry Angel, as their settlement occurred just before Christmas. Due to a delay in transferring the telephone to his new abode in Sisley Street (he ran his wireless repair business from home), he couldn't hand over the keys to BCC until the new year. Settlement had triggered a BCC rental demand to which he objected. He had anticipated 'some grace' considering the final purchase price.

The St Lucia Improvement and Debating Society wrote on 19 April 1927 to urge the Council to expedite arrangements whereby the said residents could complete their arrangements for building new homes.

The BCC accounts department's intriguing correspondence hounded Mrs Reville to maintain payments. *Trove* notes that she was the wife of Police Sub-Inspector James Reville, and that between 1928 and 1931, they hosted an annual Florin Evening Cathedral Benefit concerts in their Auchenflower home, *Te Whare*, to aid the Holy Name Cathedral building fund.

In 1931 the City Treasurer stated that:

> Mrs. C. Reville, wife of Jas. Reville...
> has failed in her obligations and promises
> to liquidate the instalments of Principal and
> Interest due to the purchase of property.

The City Treasurer reminded her on 5 April, that:

> ... arrangement was made for the systematic
> liquidation of not only your property at St
> Lucia but also the payments due to the Council
> in respect of interest and principal...in
> reviewing the account it is observed that the
> rates outstanding amount to £12.1.3 and interest
> is in arrears to the extent of £2.11.4. It must
> be understood that your account cannot continue
> in this condition and I must request...that the
> rates owing must be liquidated by instalments of
> at least £4. per month and there must be regular
> payments in reduction of the principal... unless

> payments in reduction of the principal... unless
> you see that these requirements are regularly
> complied with it is our intention not only to
> repossess the property but to take legal action
> against you for recovery of instalments in arrears.

On 30 March 1930, Mrs Reville undertook to pay £3 fortnightly, till the full amount was paid. New address c/- PO Sunnybank. The Council noted that:

> This debt was to be liquidated by 30 June 1932.

Sub-Inspector Reville took charge of Toowoomba police district in September 1930 during a colleague's holidays. He retired after 36 years' service in 1932, after extended leave. *The Courier Mail* of 26 August 1940 reported his death:

> A former police sub-inspector, Mr. James Reville,
> of Gregory Terrace, died in Brisbane yesterday.
> He retired in 1932 after having served in the
> mounted police for many years. He was also in
> charge of the Petrie Terrace police depot.

Were the couple separated? It appears Mrs Reville acted alone.

In spite of divesting much land to the Brisbane City Council, the Coronation Park Ltd was floundering before the Depression hit.

⇒ SET BACK: THE DEPRESSION ⇐

INITIALLY THE CORONATION PARK consortium to develop St Lucia seemed a promising venture. Yet who could have predicted the economic plunge that began with the Wall Street crash of 1929? Meanwhile, WA Back had sold his tasteful Mullumbimby home, Cedar House, to afford their Grand Tour of Europe.

There, in Italy, he chose and brought back to Australia the two sculptures that remained with him most of his life.

The St Lucia development was stalled by the Black Friday stock market collapse of 1929 that heralded the Great Depression of the 1930s. Eric Back continued in his memoir:

> Towards the end of the 1920s the economy started to go bad. Commodities came down in price, and my guess is Dad had a lot of farms. Some had been sold but he got them back on his hands, and each one had a mortgage to a bank. He had a very good friend, A.E. Walker on a good farm at Bangalow, and he was in the same boat as Dad. They could not sell their farms, so they went to Sydney together.

Grandad's letter of 29 January 1971 reflected on this time, together with his 'oldest living friend in Australia, Albert Walker, who is now heading for 88 years of age. After being partners together for over 20 years and traded as Back & Walker on the North Coast of NSW and Sydney':

> This included the eight or nine years of the Depression and I shall never forget those difficult times and it was a good schooling to go through, so I praise the dear Lord for having gone through that, and it gives us courage to face the future with every confidence by leaving it into the Lord's hands and under God's guidance.

–Grandad, you always find a bright side. But wasn't it tough for you and the family?

> How much tussle Albert and I had during the Depression years when we were obliged to stay in Sydney at the Hotel Arcadia many times for six weeks at a stretch, whilst Christina and Adelaide (Albert's wife) had to manage the best that they could at home with the children. So we can look back over many years of hard struggle and we can give praise to the Good Lord who watched over us and brought us safely through.

Eric Back continued:

> Dad had bought marble statues and Venetian glass in Europe and lo and behold when he was walking down George Street, Sydney, he came to an Italian Art Gallery, so he went in to compare prices. The owner was doing no good and wanted to get out at any price and Dad bought the business for very little.

Imagine what WA told his wife when he phoned home that night?

'Dear, I bought a shop full of marble statues. Indeed, we will sell and make a profit.'

He sent for Vincent [Nelson] and they sold for whatever they could get, a thousand marble clocks, dishes and statues. They even had cars going around the suburbs selling from house to house. They had to move out of George Street as the rent was too high, but they sold the lot. Dad never spoke much about the profits of this venture, but they got a lot of experience.

Cash was King of those days; those in jobs saw their pay reduced all the time. In Mullumbimby nearly every Saturday night a house caught fire when people were at the pictures. It was called selling out to the insurance company.

When people had no money the exchange business thrived, and that is what Mr. Walker and Dad were doing. It was old-fashioned horse-trading.

The Depression hit hard, and there was no past to guide people in this disaster. Every third man was unemployed and there was no dole. The Savings Bank, where poor people might have a few pounds tucked away, closed its doors. Newspapers carried advertisements like 'have savings book worth £50, will sell for £25.'

Many men were given tin dishes and a pick to go into the bush fossicking for gold, others tried to shoot kangaroos and koala bears, and a large number just carried their swags around the country, asking for police rations and handouts from property owners as they passed through. Most were well behaved, but I remember eight bagmen turned up at *Mellew* one day, asking for rations. They had a cattle dog with them, so if you knocked them back you knew they would kill sheep for themselves, use what they could, and the rest will be wasted.

OBSTACLES INTO OPPORTUNITIES

Eric continued memories of The Depression in his Memoir:

> Dad and Mr. Walker met all sorts of people on their trips to Sydney. They traded some farms to Mr. W.S. Friend in exchange for a large block of land between Parramatta and Pennant Hills. But the remarkable thing about the deed was that it was an early Land Grant to one of the discoverers of the way over the Blue Mountains, Wentworth, Lawson or Blaxland.

–Tantalising. Wish you had told us which one, Uncle Eric.

> It was a large dairy of many cows producing milk for the Metropolitan Milk Board. There was a share farmer working it; they started milking at midnight, and I suppose midday. I thought, what an awful job! When did they sleep? Dad and Mr. Walker sold in the end, but they missed a golden opportunity. After the war when Sydney grew in all directions, just one small piece of land was sold to the housing commission for over $300,000. At other times WA traded farms that he could not otherwise sell, in return for assets or produce.

At this time, they were living at the Park Farm. WA had bought it from John Morrison to subdivide the frontage into town allotments, but the Depression dampened this initiative. It was a good flat farm with a few miles' frontage to the Brunswick River, and right against Mullumbimby.

Dad exchanged the Park Farm and a Rosebank farm to Mr. Fraser for Fraser House in Sydney, and he was eventually able to sell Fraser House and end up with 14,000 in the bank! That was big money then.

In the depression there was no profit in anything. Most woolgrowers just sent their wool to the nearest selling centre and hoped for the best. Dad decided the London market had an edge on the Australian sales. Small firms favoured the London sales where they could get their purchases home in a couple of days. Dad then looked into the shipping side of things, and found most wool went in the Conference Line ships. The freight was worked out between shipping lines running regular services and the wool trade. Dad got Clarke and Tait, the biggest wool producers in Queensland to join with the Back group, as we were known then, to charter a Tramp ship to take our wool to London. The ships they chartered were not old rust buckets, but modern Norwegian diesels with a fair turn of speed. Then we saved on rail freight as they mostly loaded at Gladstone. Of course the ships had to pick up other loading on the way, and once they loaded copra and weevils got into the wool, so it had to be fumigated in London.

On one occasion Dad asked the ship if he could go along too, and what it would cost. Their answer was: 'We will give you a good cabin and take you to London, if you are prepared to pay for your meals.' The last part of this business was the selling broker in London, who happened to be Swartze, Buchanan and Co. Over the years Dad had very close relations with them. There was a constant flow of correspondence both ways, and even in the war years when wool sales ceased, Dad kept up a constant flow of food parcels to the families.

THE UNIVERSITY OF QUEENSLAND

The 'Mayne gift' was donated in 1928 but building was delayed as the founding fathers debated the ideal site for the university. A first preference was Victoria Park, close to the hospital, but construction costs would have been too expensive.

In August 1935 the Queensland Government finally committed to building the university; it announced £300,000 for the erection of buildings and, in the following year, £200,000 for their furnishing and equipment. The Premier was presented with plans for the University on 29 July, 1936 and he laid the foundation stone on 7 March, 1937, with a crowd of 2000 in attendance.

He said:

> The suburb was now in the stage of transition from gum boots (the distinguishing mark of men in the dairy yard) to horn-rimmed spectacles (the brand of the student). On the proposed University site, the St. Lucia Farm School has been temporarily established. On this farm within a city, hundreds of boys have been trained by the State to become farmers, and lads, who otherwise would be cast on the labour market, have found their vocations in life. There city boys, who previously knew nothing of Queensland beyond Queen Street, have successfully come to grips with the work of ploughing, sowing, and planting, and milking cows.

> In 1946—47 Coronation Park Ltd wound up voluntarily and the unsold land was divided among the partners. Mr Back, left with a parcel of about 40 blocks agreed to take over the sale of some of the other land of his associates.
>
> (The Courier Mail, 26 February 1936)

A negative aspect—the distance from the city centre—was countered in real estate speak with just a tiny bit of creative licence: The Town Hall Clock could be seen from Coronation Drive—now known as Hawken Drive. Strictly reading the time this way required a clear day and exceptionally good eyesight. Yet the Ironside State School timetable was set to this distant timepiece. It was described as a charming sylvan setting in some of the most picturesque country in Brisbane. After the university was built, St Lucia development expanded.

Lloyd Rees, the renowned landscape painter who lived on the far side of the river, wrote that St Lucia was infested with snakes, and 'in these areas of modest homes and far-flung farms and dairies, the children rarely wore boots or shoes to school, a few of the girls, perhaps, but for the boys—never!'

OPPORTUNITIES – YET OBSTACLES

In 1945 the remaining land, around 28 acres, was transferred to the syndicate and the title expired at that point. The post-war housing shortage opened opportunities to sell the remaining blocks. WA read widely and his eagle eyes spotted news that reinforced his plans. He wrote on 15 January 1947:

> I see by today's newspaper that New York estimates the world's shortage of housing is 100,000,000. The report adds that the shortage is primarily caused by the war and there is no more urgent problem than providing healthy and comfortable houses for the homeless.

–And who better than you to tackle this need, Grandad?

> In view of this I feel somewhat pleased with myself that I have built 70 houses in Australia, even this last one for brother KJ at Holms farm has given me a good deal of pleasure and it has not been much trouble for me.

In 1946 solders returned, de-mobilised and married. Affordable homes were being built from the Ironside State School area along Highland Terrace and Hawken Drive and towards the university. As building materials were scant they were limited to ten or twelve squares and some cheaper houses were built in fibro. As the University expanded, students were leased makeshift flats that were built under or behind houses.

In 1947, more than 400,000 British people were registered at Australia House in London in the hope of emigrating. In the early 1950s the Chifley government invited 'ten-pound Poms' to help 'populate or perish.'

After the syndicate went into voluntary liquidation in 1945–6, the brunt of development landed on WA Back's various desks. He wrote of his sense of being overwhelmed and depressed on 15 January 1947:

> I am at the crossroad. I have decided to get out of the business, also to wind up my half share with Lloyd Ellem, and everything seemed to point to a somewhat easier occupation. Wally Richards who has been retired for a long time across the river towards New Brighton has been doing his best to make a convert of me...There is certainly a lot of happiness in his countenance. He walks up leisurely to the Post Office in an open necked shirt, sandals, no socks, and to me there is nothing despisable about him...
>
> As I look over my whole life I have always got what I wanted... whether for the good or bad it has always come that way, and somehow God seemed to have given me enough faith to carry everything through... Thus would seem confirmed my definite statement that a person always gets what he wants or prays for. I am at the crossroads and have to ask myself what do I want now.

At this point, Grandad received a letter from my father Aubrey, dated 5 January 1947. Dad wrote a plaintive letter in which he complained of the outback boredom and isolation. He missed picnics at Byron Bay and the Brunswick Heads surf. 'My two hobbies are gardening, growing fruit and boat building. Both can be better done on the coast.'

> I was partly planning my future when I opened Aub's letter of the 5th January. He was contemplating putting somebody on *Hazelwood* and I seem to think I could go there. It seems such an opportunity for me to make a place there, with the most up to date and modern conveniences...
>
> I intend to contact some American architects to find out what they have in their hot climates in the way of cooling the rooms.
>
> Somebody has to start these things and I don't mind spending some time, energy and money on it. I know it is another scheme of pioneering and I seem to have been born a pioneer.

WA goes on to admit that his pioneering on the North Coast of New South Wales was a costly adventure. 'Sometimes I used to feel down hearted about it, particularly when I felt everyone was against us. All finance and departments seemed to be operating against me, but that is always the case. If one sets out to do something good he will never get much support.'

–Grandad, you sound very low, giving up. But not for long, before your vision revived.

> Meanwhile, I am just wondering about whether to go to *Hazelwood* or to take up my abode at Brunswick Heads with periodical trips to Queensland.

–Always travelling. But, Grandad, your idea to manage *Hazelwood* was short lived.

'HAZELWOOD' AND 'WILFRED DOWNS'

FOUR YEARS LATER AFTER GRANDAD'S fleeting thought bubble burst, I was born in Hughenden and lived my first decade at our property *Hazelwood* until my father bought the neighbouring *Wilfred Downs* from his sister. The sprawling homestead that he built would not have contained air-conditioning as much remained unlined.

–Grandad, how would you, even as a healthy 60-year-old, have managed the fencing, sheep mustering, shearing, dipping and crutching? Your skills lay in business.

Childhood photographs show me squinting against harsh western sun; making cubby houses in prickly bougainvillea and poisonous oleander bushes, and lined up against a fence or a Holden with siblings. The floods of memories they trigger are salty with tears. Insecurities lurked in every nook of childhood properties, like discomfort of horsehair and straw mattresses, barely contained by their ticking. After I fled a miserable Christmas gathering in my teens, I spent festive seasons in Brisbane, opting for chance lonely Passover-style left-overs instead. North-west Queensland fell off my radar.

A 2018 visit there proved healing. I was surprised by joy with the realisation that I had survived and aged stronger and was more whole than my former homes.

Hazelwood homestead blew away in a freak cyclone; only the tank stand and a shed remained. *Wilfred Downs* was immaculate when my parents moved in with their tribe of eight kids. Under subsequent absentee owners the homestead lies open and violated, abused by neglect. It disintegrated into a decrepit wasteland where Dickens and Miss Havisham might feel at home.

Doors hang a-kilter off rusty hinges. Gaping windows, festooned with spider webs, droop, exposed and vulnerable. The bath and toilet are cracked, blood-red with rust and artesian water leaks. Weeds and bindi prickles run riot on the tennis court where once we ran after balls.

In the school house we doodled all week to fathom a dozen sums, parsing and to inscribe a composition with careful loops into exercise books. They were sent by train to the Brisbane Correspondence School teacher to correct. Now, loose papers blow restless as an insomniac on a full moon.

The swing that my uncle built for his daughters lies on the dirt. The play house and sheds lurch on their stumps like drunks evicted from the pub at closing time. That date palm gave some shade until attacked by a plague of grasshoppers, who chomped, feeler to wing, along its fronds, then flew off to the next victims. Now it droops, dejected as a jilted lover.

I no longer regret the years that the locusts ate.

THE WONDROUS TELEPHONE

There were many telephone lines in the 'Big House' for WA ran teeming business operations. Grandad marvelled that he could phone his family and friends on far-flung properties and ask what rain may have fallen the previous night. He would say, 'I have been to *Landsborough, Hazelwood* and *Stockholm* stations this morning.' In an age when long-distance calls were too expensive for many people, his family — especially when he was visiting — watched vigilantly as his eyes lit upon the phone. They often tried to distract him.

This business man was careful with costs. My cousin, John Back, remembers that Grandad kept up to date with all his large family, ringing on the party lines. When the operator interrupted calls with: 'Three minutes, are you extending?' Grandad would say, 'Others will need the line,' if he was the caller. But if John rang, WA would answer: 'Yes, extension please.'

Communication was vital across such wide distances, and Grandad would drive along to check the line and repair it after floods caused damage. Many people sought his advice. His grandsons, even as experienced senior citizens, would say, 'I wonder what Grandad would do in this situation. Would he still be in the wool growing business?'

WA embraced new technologies. Kay Maxwell remembers:

> 'Mr Back was up with technology; the office had its own telex machine in the 50s–60s. It was still there when I was a child but was not used anymore. It was one of the first telexes in Brisbane, according to Mum, and other businesses would use it. Mum said (and this would have been before me) that she would go in to work in the mornings to find that things had come in from overseas during the night.
>
> I also remember the Roneo machine, which was used constantly in the late sixties and early seventies days, partly for work and partly for the church. The office was well equipped. Mum had three typewriters (plus one at home) although one was quite ancient. There were two desks, a couch and two telephones in her office. One desk was notionally Mr Back's and the other was hers but they tended to work across both. One telephone line was a direct one and the other was a shared line with Mr Nelson's office. The direct line was used for private conversations.'

TYRANNY OF DISTANCE FROM NEW SOUTH WALES

In the 1940s, during the Second World War, the army pitched tents on the portion of Coronation Drive that ran through St. Lucia. This was renamed Hawken Drive in 1950 after the death of Professor Roger Hawken, a prime mover in the development of the university.

Eric Back related in his memoir:

> Then at the other end a large area was sold to Indooroopilly Golf Club. Sometimes Dad said it was 35 acres sold for ₤3500 but it varied a bit. The company could never get ahead and the bank wanted their money, so finally it was proposed to wind the company up and share the remaining blocks between the partners... This probably made Dad and Mum decide to shift to Brisbane and Vincent Nelson sold up and came too.

WA was an astute land assessor and, after developing a swathe of Mullumbimby, the Morrison Estate, he turned serious eyes north, past the Queensland border. His business interests had expanded to the tropics, so it became a strain to divide his time between the Northern Rivers district, Brisbane and further west. Grandad often stayed at the temperance Canberra Hotel in Ann Street, Brisbane. Once he caught the bus back to his base in Mullumbimby, leaving his car standing unlocked outside the hotel. It was still there when he returned next day.

The time had come to base himself in Brisbane to enable his outreach to country areas and to focus attention on the St Lucia land. The Mayor of Mullumbimby gave WA Back a Civic Farewell on 12 September 1949. A magnificent illuminated citation, signed by the Mayor and Town Clerk read:

> *We desire to record appreciation of the progressive influence demonstrated by you as a member of this community... Your response to all charitable, public and patriotic causes has always been of the highest standard whilst every organisation and movement for the promotion and advancement of this town has benefited from your support.*

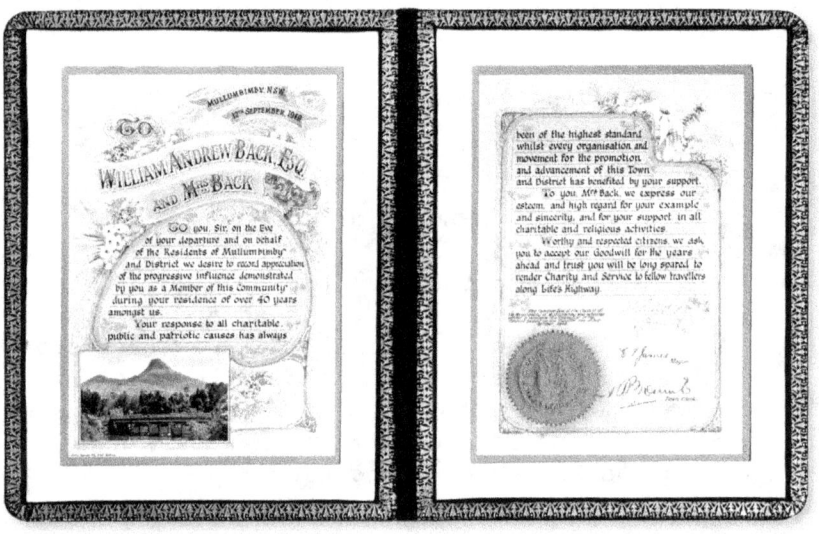

A feature article in *The Courier Mail* described WA Back as a Swede who arrived with £200 and now was building 30 rental houses and shops at St Lucia, worth more than £75,000.

```
This 63-year-old is 'affable and sprightly for
his age'; of his 50 allotments he already has
four houses partly completed in St Lucia and is
having built an ultra-modern home with lift and
```

swimming pool. It notes that building materials are obtained from Sweden, England and the Continent, bricks from Casino. All homes were equipped with hot and cold water, septic systems, and garages. Plans also included community gardens, tennis courts, and shops.

Mr. Back said his office staff would be transferred from Mullumbimby to St. Lucia and accommodated in some of the new houses.

He had built 110 houses at Mullumbimby, where he had 'carved out' 30 dairy farms from scrub land. 'Mr. Back sends his wool to London, where it has brought an average of £90 to £100 a bale this year, and twice topped the market.'

Eric suggested:

> Dad could not resist the temptation to buy land if any good blocks came on the market. He reasoned the place would come to nothing if you sat on a lot of empty land. There was no costing for each job. I would go so far as to say that he never made much money out of his building venture.

A view of the unique sunken garden with its highly decorative fountain and pool. Floodlighting facilities extend the usefulness of this most attractive area for outdoor entertaining. (Note the glass-louvred fernery in the background).

THE 'BIG HOUSE'

THE 'BIG HOUSE' OF MY MEMORIES was circled by manicured gardens. Its tiered three-storeys perched over the river like a Rhine castle, adorned by stucco ledges that were irresistible to my daredevil cousins. Did I also brave this parapet, scaredy-cat that I was? If so, terror has blotted any recollections.

Pencil pines and hydrangeas flanked the white painted front gate; we walked up the path beside a lawn garden. The front drive was classic 1950s style with a grass border surrounding a central bed. A solid balustrade and striped awning shaded the entrance from the fierce Queensland sun.

Inspired real estate PR describes an exterior wonderland at 209 Hawken Drive:

> The gardens of the 'Big House' and unique sunken garden with highly decorative fountain and pool floodlighting extends the usefulness of this area for outdoor entertaining. (Note the glass louvered fernery in the background).

–We weren't party to any outdoor entertainment, or eating in the formal dining room. Just Grandma giving us orange juice and buttered loaf in the breakfast nook. I remember the garden as being bigger, but then it didn't have a hedge. Grandad owned the whole section.

–*I always said, 'You must always own the property next door to you.'*

The back garden, flanked by palm trees, was a haven with a greenhouse and goldfish pond.

–What a poser, Grandad! Photographs in the Finnish magazine show you clowning with ferns as elkhorns, very Finnish. And seated beside the goldfish pond patting your dog. A garden pond was an eye-opener to a child from the outback. Green lawns and flowers were a tonic after dry dusty yards, and poddy sheep eating Mum's prized rose just as it came to bud.

```
A photograph shows the rear view of the dwelling
showing all three floors, the balconies to
Dining Room and Kitchen and a close-up of the
exterior entrance to the lower ground floor, a
glimpse of the lower ground floor.
```

The sliding glass door was curved around the lounge; being round, it must have been difficult to have fittings specially made. It created some decorating headaches. (Did this influence my life-long preference for the curved line to the straight?) The windows corresponded upstairs; experts have said they're difficult to replace because of the curve.

The PR brochure described it:

```
... The kitchen (which opens onto a balcony)
equipped with a fully upholstered breakfast
nook, numerous built-in cupboards and late-model
refrigerator and electric stove...The Breakfast
Nook, something right out of the ordinary in
size, comfort and decorative treatment. The
seat is fully upholstered and covered in most
attractive dark green leather.
```

–We loved to slide along that padded bench while Grandma served arrowroot or Sao biscuits with slices of tomato and cheese, or cooked sago puddings.

Nearby was the dining room where they entertained guests, including those Grandad would bring home at short notice. His long-suffering wife stretched the food around extra mouths. A cousin suggests that hospitality to potential clients was a habit learned in Grandad's real estate days, to befriend customers.

Kay Maxwell shared her mother Joan Maxwell's memories:

> Mum said that Mrs Back hated all the socialising and having strangers to the house. Mr Back was in the habit of inviting people from meetings, plus wives to the house at the drop of a hat. On many, many occasions, someone would visit the office and, at the end of it, Mr Back would say, 'Why don't you come up to the house now for lunch/tea/dinner,' driving Mrs Back to distraction.
>
> Joan and Mum had an arrangement whereby Mum would first try to rein in the invitation.
>
> 'Perhaps Mr and Mrs Smith might like to see the views at Mt. Coot-tha tonight, have a rest and come to the house tomorrow.' Mt. Coot-tha at night with Clive as Chauffeur was a favourite ploy. Failing which, she would delay the departure while calling the house to alert Mrs Back.
>
> Sometimes, your poor grandmother would end up unexpectedly having to stretch a dinner for six where she had only planned chops for two. Mum would send Clive off on an urgent mission to buy cake, biscuits, cooked food from a restaurant etc. If Clive was out on an errand (we had no mobile phones in those days) Mum would run off to Mr Browning's at high speed for emergency supplies. (Mum did not learn to drive until 1973 and always hated driving.)

At one time, there were sick visitors and Elwyn Back's wife Joan, who was also suffering from flu, had to work and provide for fourteen people. Grandad was not unappreciative of the daughter-in-law who had taken over the household running, as his wife Christina waned:

```
Joan is a wonderful disposition, calmly plodding
along and makes no arguments with anybody, what
a great gift of God. Let us try and follow that
example. I pray that my writing shall not upset
```

> you, and as before stated we will try and do all we can to help you, but we cannot do the impossible.
>
> With God's blessing to all,
>
> Dad

Joan told me that WA didn't think much about time.

–I share that with you, Grandad!

'One day I had cooked dinner, ready to serve. WA said, "Oh, some people have arrived, they'll want a cup of tea." It could be five or six or seven people. The kids were waiting to eat. Grandma helped me put the food back in the oven.'

But Joan's daughter Jenny remembers Grandma in the Mullumbimby days, as an even-tempered and capable cook, home manager and hostess to the extended Hart family who often visited.

STYLISH BEDROOMS

> Sleeping accommodation on the upper floor comprises four bedrooms, all with wall-to-wall carpeting and, in three instances, opening on to private balconies. The Master Bedroom also includes an elegant custom-built maple suite featuring twin beds and most intriguingly designed dressing table and built in wardrobes.

Such wardrobes and the winged mirrors on the dressing table were the ultimate nouveau and progressive decor for the era, as were the small washbasins in the bedrooms.

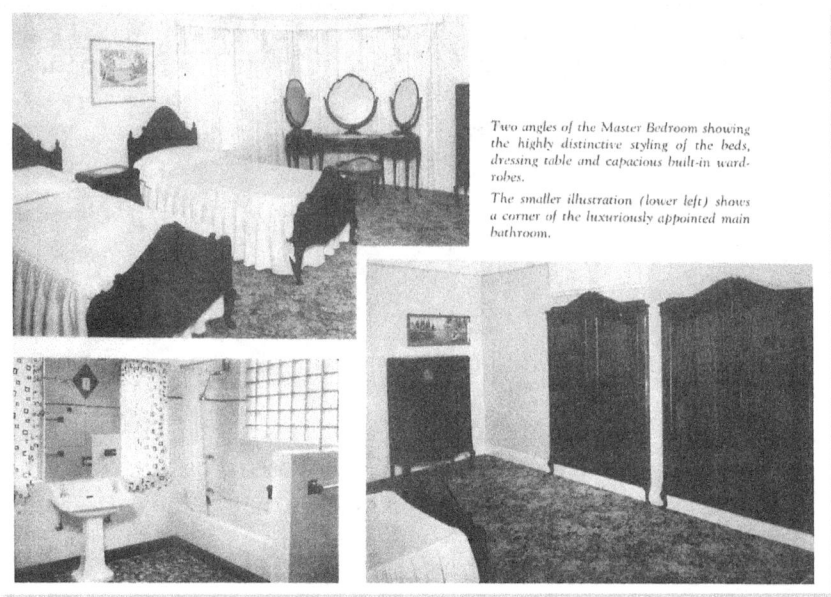

Two angles of the Master Bedroom showing the highly distinctive styling of the beds, dressing table and capacious built-in wardrobes.

The smaller illustration (lower left) shows a corner of the luxuriously appointed main bathroom.

'There was plumbing everywhere,' present owner Jane Bartlett commented. She shared that furniture was crafted by the reputed Henry Roberts.

⇒ BATHROOM ⇐

> A beautifully tiled, mirrored and appointed bathroom with toilet 'completes an arrangement to provide the ultimate in comfort and convenience for up to eight persons'.

–Grandad, you didn't spell out the wonder of the three bathroom mirrors, that they were placed at right angles so we saw multiple profiles of ourselves. These mirrors were a highlight of visits.

Jane told me that when they moved in there was a bright fire-engine red bath and basin along with faux wooden laminate. When they removed the faux rubbish they found underneath a beautiful art deco bath. They could not keep it as it had been damaged. There were art deco tiles too. Unfortunately, these could not be matched to replace damaged ones.

As a youngster, my cousin John fell asleep in the bath and didn't respond to any efforts to rouse him. He had locked the door from the inside, so Grandad had to break down the fixed ventilation louvres in the door and crawl through. Given his portly frame at the time, it was some effort. The louvres were replaced with a piece of timber, but all other doors had slats so the air conditioning could circulate.

My cousins tell the tale of when Grandad telephoned them in distress during the 1960s. 'Please come quickly, there's a woman in the bath and she won't get out.' It seems a vagrant had knocked on the door and, ever-hospitable, Grandma offered her food and drink. In her dementia, she agreed when the woman announced, 'I would like a bath.'

At least we think that's the case. Perhaps Grandma suggested a dip in the tub. The police were called to evict their uninvited guest from the bathroom.

THE ROOF GARDEN

When Michael Bryce showed me through the mansion, we solve the conundrum: 'Did I really climb onto the ledges?' From the roof top, it could be an easy manoeuvre to step onto them. Did I jump from ledge to ledge? It's possible.

My cousin Kay, Gloria's daughter, adds her own memories: 'When I was house-keeping for Grandma in 1961 I used to sunbathe up on the roof-garden, as it was euphemistically called. When the house was built I believe it must have been Grandad's intention to replicate the Italianate gardens he'd seen in their European tour of 1924, but the idea didn't transpose well to the antipodes, not to mention the glaring omission in the original design of laid-on water to the top floor! It would not have been a great expense, when the house was built, to run the pipeline up a few extra feet from the bathroom directly below but after building was completed it would have necessitated an unsightly pipe or drilling. There had been a few tubs scattered around in the beginning, but water had to be carried up in the lift and it soon became apparent that plants weren't going to thrive there without shade. That would have entailed more expense in building pergolas and Grandad's interest had moved on.'

HAWKEN DRIVE VILLAGE

WA was instrumental in creating a village hub of bank and shops nearby to his mansion. Grandad wrote on 6 March 1952 to Eric Back:

> **128 Highland Terrace**
>
> Dell Road is taking good shape now, and has forged ahead more than any other place, and we are getting the Bank of Australasia to open up in temporary premises, and the post office inspector comes out on Monday morning so we hope to finalise to get a Post Office established. I thought it best if we put up an addition for those two offices at the end of our building, it will only be three outside walls, and you will be getting some revenue for your big block then and it will pin those two buildings down to us.
>
> I have no trouble to sell the Bank of Australasia a block, and I thought perhaps the Post Office would also take a block alongside where the Bank would be building. The three blocks which we filled with the red soil, that have been bulldozed, opposite to our shopping sites should be the most suitable, so we might get a good price for those yet. It will tie the whole thing up into one block on both sides of the street in Hawken Drive. Browning is going on with his own building and also the butcher, Parnell. I sold them a block each. So when these are started it will make it a business centre, and it will save us a lot of running around when we have it at our door.

Born in 1918, Robert Elias Browning first ran a grocery store at 1 Dornoch Terrace, West End, from which he delivered goods to St Lucia. His motto was 'Bob Browning's For Better Bargains.'

Bob and his wife Helen moved into a home in Fifth Avenue in 1948 and he transported dry goods in his Dodge truck from the West End shop, and met his brother Arthur who rowed his home-made boat across the river to King's College Jetty with cold produce. In 16 years, he 'saved about 75,000 miles (112,000 kilometres) of motoring.'

In 1952, WA Back rented for £2 a week two rooms in his then Real Estate Office single storey house on Boomerang St, close to its junction with Hawken Drive. Bob and his brother knocked out garage doors to turn it into a shop. That year, Mr Back sold Lot 480, a 20 perch (506 m2), block of land for £500 to Bob Browning to enable him to build one of the first self-service stores in Brisbane.

Newspapers of the time noted there was 'entire absence of industrial activity.'

FINE NEW HOMES AT ST LUCIA

A UNIVERSITY at one end, a fine State School in the centre, and one of the best golf links in Australia at the other end—what better qualifications could any city suburb have than those?

St. Lucia—nestling between Indooroopilly and Toowong—has all those things, and these in addition:

Its land, high, yet on the river, slopes gently to the north and east, giving houses full benefit of the prevailing winds. There is an entire absence of industrial activity. That last qualification is important. It completes a sound list of requirements for an ideal residential area, and the City Planner (Mr. R. McInnis) has promised that, under his scheme to 'zone' industrial and residential areas, there will never be any intrusion of industrial undertakings into St. Lucia. Despite all these advantages and a lot more there are disadvantages, too. Years after the two estates on which St. Lucia mainly stands St. Lucia Heights and Coronation Park were subdivided for settlement in 1923, home-builders were slow in coming to settle.

There were good reasons for this. Although the site was ideal, water, gas, and electricity services had not yet been extended, to the area.

GOVERNOR'S INTEREST

Coronation Park estate had the distinction, in 1923, of being opened by the then Governor of Queensland (Sir Matthew Nathan), who, an engineer himself, praised its lay-out in exceptional terms.

The Governor was deeply interested in settlement at St. Lucia, but saw little progress there in his term of office. Because of its situation, however, people began to buy land. Even then there was a hesitancy about settlement.

Then, with modern pioneer spirit, some young couples led the way, braving the disadvantages and building their homes, services or no services. After them came other couples, and after them, in turn, came the gas and other services. Soon, the new settlers hope, will come sewerage.

The two main estates were subdivided by different surveyors, and that has resulted in a problem of conflicting roadways in some sections, but the city planner has that matter in hand. Considering its beginnings, he says, St. Lucia is still among the best-planned areas in the city.

Yet slow development has had its effect.

While St. Lucia today contains some of the best homes in Brisbane, many of them are screened so effectively by the small forests which over-run the vacant land that many a fine structure can be distinguished only by the positions of the tiled roof that may show through the trees.

While in some cases the trees really set off the homes they surround, in others there is a conflicting impression of wild undergrowth, with a beautiful cream and green stuccoed house, perhaps, standing somewhere in the background.

Though the services have come to St. Lucia, as yet the city's network of bitumen roadways has not yet extended through it. Some of the homes are surrounded by dusty, rough roadways bordered by unkempt shrubbery and disordered dry grass.

But the home-builders are winning the battle against the trees, the grass, and roads.

Nowhere else in Brisbane, excepting, perhaps, Ascot and Hamilton, could one find whole streets of such modern homes, each house containing features ideally suited for the Australian climate.

'QUEENSLAND' HOMES

Here, Queensland architecture is being developed 'in the mass,' heralding the day, perhaps not far off, when St. Lucia will be referred to as a 'show suburb.'

Timber and brick have been used equally effectively in the fine homes on the heights, bordering the river and leading down to the new university. Cream, with touches of green, forms the basis of the colour scheme of most of the homes, but among the cream dwellings in some streets, are homes in solid brown brick.

Tiled roofs add a further dash of colour to the gay aspect of the settled areas.

> Interior comfort has not been sacrificed for modernity in most of the homes. Over-hanging roofs are featured in many houses, protecting the walls from the summer sun, and window shades and veranda awnings are prominent in the designs.
>
> St. Lucia has been slow to develop, also, because of its distance from the city, over the roundabout route through Toowong and Auchenflower. Though it is now well-served by a bus run, most of the residents are car owners.

In 1953, after three year's planning and building, the St. Lucia shops were nearly completed, designed in American style by Cramphorn and Millin, builders and part-owners. Mr Cramphorn said the total cost of the shops and service station would be about £15,000. 'The block will contain a smart American-style grocery shop, [with] big windows to give the customer a better view of the shop's whole interior, chemist, dressmaker, butcher, cake and fruit shops, ladies' hairdresser, builders' and hardware store, and either a newsagency or bank branch, petrol station.' The new shopping centre would mean that housewives would not have to make long shopping trips. It would also serve the University colleges to be built nearby.

Bob Browning opened the first shop in 1952 and, by the 1960s, it had evolved into a self-service supermarket, one of the first in Brisbane. I remember our wide eyes when, rather than stand in front of a counter and wait to be served, we could push a trolley ourselves and choose items from the shelves. Bob always wore a white apron and a smile. Next door was the ANZ bank; both began in a white timber house. WA promised the ANZ bank a lot of accounts, so they opened up part-time. Decades later my husband and I returned after seven years in Europe. With little banking history, our hopes of buying a house were slim until the bank manager noted: 'Oh, you're William Back's grandchild?' and the loan process was fast-tracked.

Kay Maxwell, who grew up in St Lucia wrote:

Mr and Mrs Back employed a housekeeper and gardener. At one point, it was Mr and Mrs Ive—Giuseppe and Maria. Giuseppe was an artist and supplemented this with other jobs, including house painting. He painted the mural in the garage of the Hawken Drive house and there is (or was) a large painting by him hanging in the dining area of the Irish club in Brisbane. He used to do the Italian float in the Brisbane Spring festival each year.

The couple lived in the ground floor flat and later built a red brick house in Dell Road, on the corner of Mavis St. As Mr Ive's painting career took off, he stopped doing other jobs and had his studio in Dell Road.

My mother's sister and her husband, Clive Stone, built a house at 108 Dell Road, where the old supermarket carpark was. They lived there until about 1962-ish when the marriage broke up. Norma was an accomplished singer and worked part-time at the University. Next door to them, at number 112, there lived Nat Kipner and his family. Nat was an American musician who had met his wife when he was a soldier during the war. He played the piano at a cinema in the city and he and Norma were engaged in various musical pursuits around town and on early TV.

Nat later went on to run a record company in Australia and later composed a number of hit songs. His son, Steve Kipner was also a musician and wrote *Physical* for Olivia Newton John. At one point, Steve was in a band with Carl Groszmann (known professionally as Carl Keats). Carl flatted with Ringo Starr in London, post-Beatles, and they worked together.

Carl was a cousin of Colin Keats, a singer, pianist and well known singing teacher in Brisbane. He is still alive and living in Taringa. Colin is also Mum's cousin.

St Lucia in the 1960s had four churches, two schools, a Bowls Club, and a Golf Club.

GETTING AN EDUCATION

THE DILEMMA OF SCHOOLING for the children of families on outback stations is often intense for parents. Many take the boarding school solution; which providence allowed me to avoid.

Grandad was behind my education at Ironside State School in St. Lucia. He knew that my mother didn't want to send all the family to boarding school. Four of my siblings had travelled by train to schools in Charters Towers and returned with long, glum faces. Townsville would have been a closer option to commute between our properties *Hazelwood* and *Wilfred Downs*, outside Hughenden—365 miles by train as opposed to 1000 miles by car to Brisbane, much of that over dirt roads until the bitumen appeared at Roma.

I wonder how my life might have evolved if I had been schooled in Townsville, where my maternal grandparents lived. They owned a block of four units on The Strand, looking over the sea to Magnetic Island. But the Townsville option was shunted aside and Mum's plans were changed when her father-in-law offered our family his house on Highland Terrace.

When I was five, and on the brink of starting school, Grandad wrote of his bad experience buying a desert property:

> 26th November, 1956
>
> Dear Helen and Aubrey,
>
> None of us want to domineer your family or dictate what you should do in bringing up the family or giving them the necessary education but I can say that although I was hard-pressed from 1914 when I bought 'Rocklea' my first consideration was for our young family and after surveying it from all angles I could not see the wisdom of bringing you north to 'Rocklea', so I and your mother felt the only thing was to continue with the schooling at Mullumbimby.

—Um, forgive my saying so, Grandad, but more commas and periods would clarify your letters. Of course, you dictated to Joan Maxwell, and she typed as you spoke.

> I don't see that Mullumbimby school was anything exceptional but it was the best or as good as anything going at the time. Yes, parents have certain obligations and care which should be extended to the children and if Helen doesn't favour the idea of sending them to boarding school I think she should be the best judge of that as she had that boarding school experience...
>
> This brings us back again to Highland Terrace, so what about it? I know there is always a lot for and against so don't carry on arguing just start from where the possibilities begin and build up something, but when you are floundering from one thing to another I am sure that it cannot give you peace of mind nor will there be any real blessing in it. Yes, let's just keep to number one resolution—the house was intended for Helen, Aubrey, and the family.
>
> Now that it becomes empty let us give some constructive thoughts to it... Let me tell you

there is no trouble to give the house away, there is no trouble to re-rent it again and we can sell it as there has been so much inquiry about it and Mr. Payne the agent has been is calling on me and ringing me up practically every day...

I would like to make it known that this was not a given as an investment, it was intended for a home, and a home to my mind is not to be counted as an investment or money making proposition.

Yes, if you give Highland Terrace a try out now with an earnest desire to give the children schooling perhaps some other helpful means may come to your assistance. Would it be impossible to get some matron to come and keep house for them when you are absent at *Hazelwood*? All these things have to be tried out. I don't say that I can solve it for you but let us say like the prophet of old 'come let us reason it out together.'

Yes, it was given to you for a home and that doesn't say then that you must get there, no we don't want to impose this 'must'. You have already stated that you would like to live in Townsville so therefore if that is going to be more congenial and more suitable if you buy a place there and this can be sold to pay for it. I don't see why Townsville would be any better than Brisbane, except if Mr. and Mrs. Lord would be living there, but we have to make some arrangement.

It would be unfair to keep these people in Melbourne waiting until January and not let them have the house. We must give them a definite answer one way or the other. Houses are hard to get, in fact it was on account of this housing shortage that we started to build here and that house shortage has never eased up. In fact, most agents say that it is harder than ever now, and should there be any further trouble or war that seems to just make it almost impossible to get houses as there is so much influx of populations coming to the towns and cities.

So it was that this letter paved the way for me to come to St Lucia.

This shy outback child had to don a grey pinafore uniform, white blouse and sandals, pack her 'port' with a vegemite sandwich and apple, and walk with brothers the kilometre or so to the big Ironside State School. There, staccato orders of 'answer down' and 'hands on heads' paralysed my brain. I kept scribbling after the volley fire second command. Stilt dinosaur legs bore down on me. Headmaster Mr Murray's manacle hand pounced. Freakish long arms lifted me aloft by my collar. I flinched from his yellowed parchment skin and sour hot breath and tuba-bellowed rebuke.

My mind has been a blank on arithmetic since.

At 'big lunch', jeering children terrified me. Like dogs and horses, they sensed my fear. Rather than brave the hopscotch or Jungle Jim climbing frame and swings, I found sanctuary in the toilet block. Or I wandered around the vast asphalt oval, throwing listless swings of my yoyo. I wore that vacant fixed smile of the loner that says, 'I'm fine, quite happy by myself, thank you.'

After a torrid day at the Big School, I sought a haven in a brocade armchair in the 'Big House'. Grandad jiggled me on his pneumatic lap and soothed my shattered esteem by calling me his 'bestest little girl'—later, I realised, so were all his granddaughters. But the words poured balm into my troubled little soul.

Ironside State School plunged me into a whirlpool out of my depth, yet invited me to swim in uplifting, invigorating waters that would refresh my future life. My education path through it to Somerville House and onto the University of Queensland would open wide horizons to travel the world; to study, work and live in Europe for seven years. If I had been educated in Townsville, would I have married a grazier instead of a musician? Would I then have been faced with that same quandary regarding the education of our children?

UNIVERSITY OF QUEENSLAND

WA VALUED EDUCATION AND ENCOURAGED the idea of moving the University of Queensland campus from Gardens Point in central Brisbane out to St Lucia. He enabled my own education through giving my family the home at 160 Highland Terrace so we could attend Ironside State School, and later UQ. He was proud of his granddaughters who obtained degrees.

–Though, Grandad, did you really say 'Universities turn out a lot of educated idiots'?

– *I spoke and wrote so many words, I cannot remember them all.*

–Or warn family that offspring 'could be smitten with that curse which comes from that higher education'? Such discouragement shows a lack of faith in your descendants' good sense.

–*Fundamentalist church youth leaders warned young people to not attend university in case they might 'lose their faith.'*

–Their minds were small as mustard seeds and they expected us to be similar. They should have trusted Christ to nurture our faith from that mustard seed to fruition.

The house at 160 Highland Terrace was about a half-hour walk from the Music Department in the basement of J.D. Story Administration building. Or a twenty-minute run, if I was late, so my daily glimpse of the 'Big House' was fleeting.

This home gave us haven until 1971 when my siblings readied their wings to fly the nest elsewhere. Our parents battled a bitter drought out west and had little time to visit. Grandad sold the house on the family's behalf. The flotsam of decades of living was packed off to charities. Few of us had the time, energy or inclination to sort it out. I moved into Grace College—women's residential facilities close to the University of Queensland—where meals appeared three times a day with no effort of shopping, cooking or washing dishes.

In recent decades I chose to drive to the University of Queensland via Hawken Drive rather than Coronation Drive, slowing along Highland Terrace to peer at my former home. A white fence blocked my view, but one day it was open and a tradesman's utility parked inside. How could I resist a brake and enter attempt? Calls and knocks. No response. I ventured into the front garden, where once we played 'Red Rover Come Over' on green grass, now paving and cement sprinkled with weeds.

A grille door swung wide open like a drunken sailor on uneasy hinges. Yawning holes gaped in the ceiling above the locked glass entrance door and porch. A 1960s photo shows three sisters posed there in their Sunday best, wearing hats, gloves and stockings.

Red bougainvillea and brambles now thrive on the vegetable scraps my mother lovingly dug into her rose garden, in the days before composting became de rigeur. Shutters now shield windows of the side bedroom where my sister and I argued over who should get out from under our mosquito nets to switch off the light. That sun deck—where we picked luscious pawpaw and fed kookaburras—has been enclosed. Units now squeeze into a stony gulley, on which brothers zoomed billy-goat carts down a break-neck steep hill.

A side entrance gate swings an open invitation so I sneak down to the back door steps. Every night Mr. Redhead the milkman climbed these, calling, 'Good night, good night!' to pour milk, still warm from his cows at Long Pocket into our jug.

The house next door seems, from the outside, little changed. A Chinese family lived there during our time. They were quiet, industrious, upstanding people.

–Grandad, talking of the Chinese, I don't know if I should quote your letter of 20 May, 1959, written when our family had moved back to our property *Hazelwood* after two years' schooling at Ironside State School. How you brought to 160 Highland Terrace a potential buyer or lessee, the Vice-Consul for America, 'in his shiny car'.

```
As I expected the tenants to be away at the
University I quietly prepared him for a
preliminary inspection from the outside. We walked
around but I am sorry to say we did not get a very
good impression of the place. I am not going to
start to condemn anybody but when there is nothing
done to a place, two months can make it very dirty
and untidy.

I felt very despondent and thought that we would
just quietly walk away, as the blinds were drawn
and the doors closed. But evidently Mr. Mills
had better hearing and he said, 'I think there
is somebody inside.' So I pressed the button and
after a while a shy-looking Chinese half-opened
the door, stuck his head round the corner and
asked, 'What do you want?' At first he did not
want to let us in, but the principal came to the
door, so I told him that I thought the two months
were up and that we had given them notice to quit.
```

–So far no issue. He asked if our family would return and needed it ourselves. But then you 'gathered some courage and pushed in.'

```
As we were walking through the hallway the
Chinese heads bobbed up everywhere in every
door. It was just like disturbing an ant's nest,
```

they were coming from all directions. I didn't know how many would have been there, but we both realised we were in a real Chinese den... We did not get into the sleeping rooms downstairs...

After yesterday's episode I feel I just want to rest from it all and not allow myself to think about anything—just praise the Lord for all the experience that we have had, and leave it to the Lord to guide us in the future.

WOMEN IN THE WORKPLACE – A FORWARD THINKER

WA BACK WAS PROGRESSIVE IN his support for women's rights, reputedly having correspondence with Doris Lessing, whose 1962 book *The Golden Notebook* posed challenging questions like: *What is a woman for? What is her destiny? Does she get to choose it?*

It put into print the resentment, frustration and anger that many women felt, unable to use their skills beyond marriage and maternity.

Australian women attained suffrage before most countries — in 1901. They first voted in 1902. Finland was soon after, in 1906, the first European nation to do so.

Finland led the world to initiate female rights, so women continued to work after bearing children. Leaders included Tekla Hultin, who became one of the first female doctors, and Rosina Heikel and Lucina Hagman who, in 1892, had formed the *Unioni* and the Martha Organisation, similar to the Country Womens' Association in Australia.

It's no surprise then that my grandfather was innovative in supporting women in the workplace, even though Australian laws were less progressive when it came to employment of married women.

For nearly 40 years, WA relied on his efficient right-hand-woman Joan Maxwell to run the office and type his stream of consciousness dictation. I remember her as auburn haired, high-heeled chic.

Her daughter Kay Maxwell remembers:

> Mr. Back needed a secretary. I am not sure whether he already had someone or if Mum was the first—I suspect not. But, he spoke to the headmaster to see if there were any likely girls who were about to finish school. (Mullumbimby school only went to Junior at that time.) The Headmaster offered a few names, none of which impressed WA. But, he did say that Joan Attewell would be finishing senior at Murwillumbah soon and might be looking for work, pending College.
>
> WA remembered Mum, knew the family and thought it might work. Mum was invited in for a chat, during which she was offered the job. She said that she wanted to go to teacher's college as soon as she was old enough (Mum finished senior

at 14, having been advanced through a number of grades). WA agreed that she would work for him for the next few years. Apparently, there was a bit of jealousy around town at the time as working for WA was considered a plum role.

Working in the early years

Mum never went to teacher's college, choosing to stay on in the office with Mr. Back. She found the job interesting and loved meeting, talking and corresponding with such a vast range of people. Like Mr Back, Mum was very social and loved the busy environment.

Initially, her work life was confined to Mullumbimby. She knew the Back family and grew fond of Mr and Mrs Back and the children, most of whom were older than her. She said that she didn't get to know many of them well until she was older as they went to live out west early on. She knew Alan, the youngest, well at this time. He would pop into the office during holidays, and spend far too much time chatting to her as she tried to go about her job. At one point, Mr Back tried to encourage a romance there but Mum said that Alan was like a brother and neither of them were interested in the slightest. That was one deal, she said, Mr Back was not able to close.

Mum worked five full days and a half day on Saturdays. Mr Back had a stock and station agency so she would be working busily all Saturday morning, longing for the 1pm close so that she could go to tennis. The farmers would come to town and do their shopping, stopping at the office for a chat once the shops closed. Mum could not leave until they did so was often late for tennis.

Mr Back's brother Karl Johan would often also pop in for a chat. Mum thought he was lovely, though rather eccentric. He used to spend hours explaining to her all sorts of plans for the country and political opinions. Mum thought he was a little lonely.

Mr Back had a friend in Canberra who ran Hansard. Mum had met him on several occasions in Sydney and he suggested that she might like to go to Canberra to work for him. Mr Back was not happy but said that it would be a good for her career. She thought that she would miss her mother too much (and possibly Dad too as they were courting at the time) so decided against it.

As well as going to Sydney, Mum spent some time in Brisbane over this period. Mr Back had property interests in Brisbane and was working on an estate development in St. Lucia. And, of course, there was the wool and lobbying to do. In Brisbane, Mum would stay with her aunt, Rose Keats née Locke, or at the Hotel Canberra. Mr Back liked this hotel as it was temperance.

Mr Back would take people out to lunch at a Chinese restaurant in Fortitude Valley. It had several levels and the higher up you went, the fancier and more expensive it was. They always went to the top level. Mum went to many of these lunches with Mr Back.

The development at St. Lucia was going slowly and that was a large part of the reason for the move to Brisbane. Mr Back felt that if he was there permanently, things would hop along.

When the decision to move was made, Mum was going too. By this point, she had been with WA for 10 years and loved her work and (most) of the people. Mum's mother decided to sell up and move to Brisbane too. Her sister also came. Mum's brother finished an apprenticeship in Mullumbimby and came as well.

Brisbane real estate was more expensive than in Mullumbimby so the house at 120 Dell Rd (in between Mrs Oakes and Mrs Mountcastle—another Northern Rivers person and a distant relation of Dad's) was bought by my grandmother, uncle and Mum in 1950. The house was built by Roy Kohnke. Mr Walters (another Back employee) moved across the road. Mr Back gave Mum the profits from a bale of wool to help her into the house.

Their office at St Lucia was initially in a building on the corner next to the supermarket. It was mostly glassed across the front—the glass shattered when they had an earth tremor at one point. They were there until they moved into The Esplanade. The original office came down and was replaced with a petrol station (there were two of these at one point in St Lucia—the other owned by a Mr Cross, I think, a former race car driver.) A real estate agent in St. Lucia who was selling WA Back's old office on The Esplanade told that the old safe (a bank sized number under the house) is still there as is the staircase that used to go from the office up to the house—although she says that it is not useable now.

At the back of 120 Dell Rd, there was a creek. This was dammed up to build the old shopping centre but springs would pop up at the bottom of the garden in heavy rain.

Going back to work

Mum planned to be a stay-at-home mother after my birth. She only had one child, myself, in 1963 at the age of 37—after 23 years working with WA. Mum left work one week before I was born. She had organised for the wife of someone (can't recall who but a friend of W.A. or someone in the family) to take on the job. The lady in question had worked at a senior level and was thought to be a good fit. It was now the 1960s and a number of married women were pursuing careers!

Mum was in hospital for two weeks after having me. After the birth, flowers arrived and one week afterwards, so did WA. He could not work with that woman, he said. She did not understand him and was irritating. She had made a lot of mistakes. Please come back, he said. Women in Finland keep their careers after having children and Mum should do this too. They could work around the baby.

So, three weeks after I was born and a week after Mum and I left the hospital, Mum and WA were working from our lounge room. WA brought stationery, typewriters, furniture, including a comfy chair for him and an office chair for Mum, over from the house/office and Dad built a desk for them to use. So, for the first 5 years of my life, our lounge room doubled as an office. We didn't have a telephone so any calls were made and received through the phone next door (Mrs Oakes, the mother of Joan Back). WA would be dropped off by Clive Stone (his Chauffeur and the former husband of Mum's sister, Norma) most mornings to sort out correspondence and then be collected to go home to the big house for lunch.

After lunch, Mr Back would come back if signatures were required. He would often fall asleep for a nap in his chair. He would have been in his sixties at this time.

As late as the 1960s, women were expected to resign when they married, and even more so, if they became pregnant. Iconic feminist Merle Thornton concealed her marriage and pregnancy even though:

> '…Any female employee discovered to have married and to have kept this from the public service, as I had, according to Section 49 (2) of the *Commonwealth Public Service Act*, "shall be deemed to have retired from the Commonwealth service upon her marriage." As with the stats clerks, these women promptly lost their jobs. I had been far naughtier than that poor woman: I had concealed my marital status from my employers for two and a half years. And now, fronting up after Christmas, there was no mistaking the bun in my oven… I confessed as I had to, though I wanted to keep working as long as I could. I enjoyed my job and felt I made a real contribution there. I was hugely resentful at having to resign, but resign I did. I said goodbye to a job I loved and turned to motherhood, something entirely new and completely overwhelming.'

–Thank you, Grandad, on behalf of other women, for making practical solutions to keep your secretary in work and for working around her child.

Thornton tackled other inequities. In April 1965 she surfed the wave of protest after she and a friend chained themselves to the Regatta Hotel Bar in Toowong, to protest that women were forbidden to drink alcohol in public bars. She was a keen observer of the social unrest that went with this exclusion: 'I saw indigenous people getting about town, doing their own thing, something I had not once seen in the three other capital cities I have lived in; and in the evenings outside pubs I saw queues of parked cars with women and fractious pyjama-clad children trying to retrieve dad and take him home—at times they even crowded on the footpath and in the dark. Further south the six o'clock swill still existed, but in sweltering Brisbane the pubs were open until 10 pm. This often meant blokes missed their dinner.'

After the success of this protest Thornton held the Equal Opportunities for Women inaugural meeting in April 1965. 'I proposed that its fundamental aim was to get rid of the public service marriage bar.'

As far back as 1958, the recommendation of the Committee of Inquiry into Public Service Recruitment, otherwise known as the Boyer report, was unequivocal:

> 'That married women shall be eligible for permanent or temporary employment in the Service... This results, for example, in the situation that a permanent typist on marriage is re-employed as a temporary typist but a professional officer is not re-employed to continue her professional work, and so is lost to the Service.'

Not good enough, decided Thornton and her colleagues.

This was a time when organisations didn't have gender politics—the word 'gender' wasn't used in that manner at the time (even the term 'male chauvinist' is only thought to have come into use in the late 1960s.)

On 29 October 1966 the Queensland parliament passed a bill that secured women's rights to work after marriage. No longer must they opt to 'live in sin' or else be fired.

Kay Maxwell continues:

> During her time with Mr Back, Mum became very fond of him, Mrs Back and the whole family. But her first allegiance was always to "WA". She found him to be a kind and progressive employer. Over the years, they shared their worries and stories and sought each other's counsel in times of trouble. Mum said that he was like an uncle to her.
>
> Despite his success and, on occasion, ruthlessness (Mum used to say that no-one ever got the better of him in a deal) in business, he was supportive of those in trouble or needing a friend. He was gregarious and outgoing, having a wide circle of friends and acquaintances where Mrs Back was a shy lady who preferred her home.

Joan Maxwell worked for WA Back from late 1939 until 1977, three years after his death. She stayed on to wind up the estate. She said they handled the business of 96 properties at one point. She had qualified as an accountant, encouraged by WA, but she hated it. She loved the charity work, and that was one of Grandad's fortés. She recalled him as a major influence on her life.

> I grew up alongside him from the time I was a baby. My mother Joan Maxwell worked in his office as secretary—but much more—for 36 years. Mr Back was a prolific and keen correspondent. Mum would type his letters as he spoke. Sometimes, he would record his thoughts on a reeled recording device and Mum would have to make sense of directions like: 'I want you to write to x and tell him that I am not happy to do y.' But mostly, she would type as he spoke. I remember listening and he did not speak slowly. She typed as he was conversing so grammar and punctuation would have been Mum's guess as she went along.
>
> Mr Back often wrote letters in Swedish. Mum was good with languages. I didn't realise how good until I travelled with her

in the 1980s and found that she was fluent in French and quite good in Italian—both learned in her youth and practised on friends over the years, also a little German.

Working for WA, she acquired basic conversational Swedish. It helped that her best friend, Ellen Fors—a Swede who came to Australia and settled in Mullumbimby—was happy to converse with her. Mr Back would dictate letters in Swedish and Mum would type. Often, he would use words that she did not know and she would say, 'How do you spell that?' He would say 'I can't remember—you can guess it.' Other times, he would stop and say, 'What is the word for "conundrum"?'

'How would I know that?' she would ask.

'Well, put it in anyway. They will work it out.'

Mrs Back was lovely but vague. Mum used to pop up to visit her when she was still at the house. Mum was very fond of her—she was a quiet and sincere person. I think she was accepting and supportive of WA's approach to life. I can't remember when they left the Big House but the Vice Consul was a tenant there in the early seventies.

BENEFACTOR OR A SOFT TOUCH?

WA Back was rumoured to be a millionaire, but his estate incurred death taxes, only abolished two years after his death in 1976. With many bequests to charities and missions, his executors scratched to find funds to cover these, so there was little bounty for his vast, extensive family.

Did Christina struggle to budget? A cousin noted Christina was very frugal in putting the food on the plates, there were nutritious home-cooked meals but small portions.

–I gave money to many, to help them begin their new lives. Some paid me back when they could.

–I have heard many stories of your generosity. You wrote a letter sending £50 to a Balkan refugee.

Having grown up poor and now living with conspicuous wealth, Grandma was afraid of robbery. Was it dementia that she often hid things? Or did she revisit her childhood? They searched and searched for Grandad's watch until one day, while putting clothes away in the socks drawer, WA picked up a sock. It was heavy. Grandma had hidden his money there. Once he found a roll of notes in a shoe.

'Did you hide this money?' he asked.

'No.'

'Well, I left some money on the dressing table. I supposed you spent it?'

'I thought some burglar might come in and rob us.'

My cousin John noted: 'Whenever we were leaving, Grandad pulled out his wallet and gave the older kids a pound each and younger ones got ten shillings.'

As a reputed millionaire, many came to ask WA for financial aid. A benefactor to many, was WA a soft touch? One who couldn't say 'no'? He was alert to needs within the family, especially those in war-torn Finland. He shipped food packed in calico, with clear instructions:

'Parcels have to be perfectly packed otherwise they squash up and the syrup and custard powder get mixed and spoiled. There must be a terrific weight on the bottom parcels in the ships. So therefore it is no wonder that some of my parcels have been badly damaged.'

WA wrote to his sister Sofia and niece Helmi in Finland in December, 1956:

> I have already posted your Christmas cards and I enclosed a £5 pound note in each. This is not permissible and I suppose I should not do it. But at Christmas time we feel that we like to give people a little cheer and what else can we send. I know money is always useful.
>
> Again with our best wishes for a happy Christmas and a peaceful 1957.

John Back says:

> Grandad wrote often, especially when I was at boarding school, and he'd include a £1 note—riches in those days, so my school mates thought I was king! We received many coloured postcards that folded out when he travelled overseas.

PATRIARCH AND FAMILY MAN

WA loved children. He urged his daughter and daughters-in-law to have more babies.

As I enjoy the opportunities to bond with my own grandchildren I ask myself:

What did my grandfather pass on to me? How do I express it to my grandchildren?

A favourite book is *Going on a Bear Hunt,* and we term our picnic walks bear hunts. I muse that we can't go over it, we can't go under it. We have to go through it. In my past, when confronted with a brick wall, I would go around it. Take a detour; another tangent might succeed where the last path stalled.

WA assumed the role of patriarch as his older brother Karl Johan was a reclusive bachelor.

Cousin Jenny, the eldest of our generation, gives her memories about our mutual grandfather:

> He was a very generous man. When he heard that I was born and all was well he was most happy. Some man was with him in his Mullumbimby office at that moment with a hard luck story and asking for some help. Grandad said he straight away handed him some money, in celebration. He would tell me that I cost him money as soon as I was born.
>
> Grandad often had calls from people asking if they could have an appointment to see him and ask for advice. He seemed to be willing to help with advice but the 'appointment' was difficult for him to come to terms with.
>
> 'How do I know when I will be available?'
>
> Grandad would discuss business (and sometimes religion) for hours. I don't think he ever talked down to my Dad, Elwyn or took advantage of his experience. He put much thought into other people's financial troubles. On visits to properties in the west he would often come back mulling over a problem. He would have tried to help in one way or another. Sometimes he would be worried that there was conflict in the families where he had been.

Grandad loved children and grew more indulgent with age.

```
11 December 1947

Yes, give the children the toys before Christmas.
No doubt children are a wonderful link between
heaven and earth and to see the children happy
makes the grown-ups also happy. With the
Christmas season, we want to give the children
all the happiness that we can and it pays the
```

> best dividend of all—when they are happy it makes us happy, and when we get a contented mind it is a heavenly joy within our souls. I think that demonstrates the true Christmas spirit. God loved us first and therefore it is that love which begets more love and where there is love there can be no friction or dissatisfaction.

Kay Maxwell reflects on influence that WA Back had on her life.

The answer is a work ethic and the importance of kindness. These things also came from my mother but I think that she and Mr Back shared a similar world view after so many years. When I went to the office over school holidays, Mr Back would find jobs for me to do—things like tidying up and sorting cupboards, making cups of tea, addressing and stuffing envelopes, popping up to the shops for supplies, taking the mail to the post office and so on. Each week over the holidays, I would get a pay packet—a little buff coloured envelope—the same as the others with a few dollars in it. I was a saver and Mr Back used to commend my efforts.

Some of my hard earned dollars did go to books though as I was, and still am, an avid reader. Over the holidays, I would read anything I could get my hands on—including the romances that Colleen (Mr Nelson's daughter) liked to buy, like Georgette Heyer. I learned to read very young—I could read by the time I was 4. Mum said that she taught me to give me something to do while she worked. I could read and write quite well by the time I started school. Mr Back was a great source of religious texts; children's books about Jesus when I was small.

Mr Back was also a kind man, generous of spirit and forgiving of others' weaknesses. This also made an impression on me.

He also loved lollies. He really liked the false teeth ones and would put them in his mouth and wear them about to amuse me. He loved them so much that I remember asking Mum for extra cents to buy Mr Back a bag of his own.

A MAN OF FAITH

MUNSALA CHURCH WAS HUGE for such a village. The plans for its construction had been confused with those of Nykarleby, a larger parish. It was finished in 1635 after a hundred years of work given by the farmers of the village in their spare time. My great-grandfather Anders Karlsson Ohls Back was a church warden for some time.

Before Grandad emigrated from Finland, his brother KJ wrote in an undated letter around 1900:

> To my brother, Wilhelm,
>
> Looking at my father's letter I see that you are going in the school and intend to study to become a priest.

He then went on to urge his brother to emigrate and the idea of priesthood was dropped, as were many of WA's bright ideas, like becoming a missionary in China. This might have been in the 1950s before the Cultural Revolution.

Cousin Betty reported that Grandad would read Bible stories to her and sister Dawn when they were primary school age. He and Grandma read their devotions daily; sometimes he spent a whole day in his pyjamas, praying and reading the Bible.

My cousin Kay recalls the Billy Graham Crusades of 1959 'and the lengths Grandad went to in order to make sure my cousins and I were able to hear him. Afterward the rally he arranged for Billy Graham's brother-in-law Leighton Ford to come back to the

"Big House" for supper, where we girls had a photo taken with him showing us a passage of Scripture in the Bible. (That was a highlight of my boarding school days!)'

Several cousins remember the lengthy prayer sessions spent on knees beside him while he prayed for all the family by name—forty-five minutes on one occasion as our family was large!

WA would rise as early as 5 am, brew tea and bring bread and butter up to Grandma and the family. One cousin remembers that he brought her freshly squeezed orange juice at 3 am, after which he would read the newspapers and his Bible, before breakfast around eight. At 9 am the whole family listened to Radio 4BC Morning Devotions with Rev Vernon Turner, so it was late before the day started going. A 1960s interview with Vernon Turner, transcribed from reel-to-reel tape, begins by saying, 'You're looking well, Mr Back' to which he answered:

> And why shouldn't I be? Nothing to care about, everything is cared for me, if I didn't have a Lord and saviour to guide and direct us it wouldn't be anything to confess but when you confess Him as your guide and your protector and your keeper there's nothing you have to add to it is there?
>
> When I look back about my sinful life I just doubt myself but then St Paul said to not look back over the past at all but just look forward, go forward.
>
> I don't want to be a preacher but I just want to tell people about some of my mistakes in order to save them from making the same mistakes which I have done all through my life. The main thing is to believe in the Lord Jesus Christ and to confess him to keep to his commandments. Hasn't he told us that 'if we keep His commandments and do it I and my father will come and take our abode with us'? I think that's the greatest promise what we can have, to have Christ in you the hope of glory.

Grandad quoted Martin Luther:

'It is a great matter when in extreme need to take hold on prayer. I know, whenever I have prayed earnestly, that I have been amply heard, and obtained more than I prayed for. God indeed sometimes delays but at last He came.'

I was meditating on this quotation and my mind went back right to the depression years. A period which has certainly made an indelible mark in my memory and no doubt in your memories too, as you all went through it with me. Yes, it was a period of great struggle and I remember praying for different ways of getting out of Morrison Park, Mullumbimby and Coronation Park, Brisbane, as both these subdivisions seemed to be such a complete failure. And of course from time to time I thought out different schemes how to solve it, but now as I look back over all those proposals put forward by myself to the Lord I must honestly say that anything that I had in mind was far short of the blessing which the Good Lord brought forward in the appointed time.

... The Coronation Park had a much better ending than whatever I or any of us expected it to have financially and otherwise. But in the long run we did receive some financial gain and will I say blessing from it and it was all God's doing—not our own.

Each day seems to bring its particular problem, but if we look closely into it from another angle there is always some blessing mixed with each day that we are granted to live. Let us learn to accept it as such and gladly do what we can from day to day.

Brisbane City Council Archives website

DROUGHT AND FLOODING RAINS

The cycle of drought and flood is as old as our continent. WA was both encouraging and challenging to his sons experiencing difficulties in dry, drought-stricken Queensland.

He wrote to family many encouraging missives such as this of 3 December 1952:

> No doubt having gone through so many droughts before you can keep up the courage and that is the main thing in life and no matter how bad one day might open up it is something of the other side always blended with it. I mean there is always something good with every bad news. Out of each problem and difficulty there is something behind it which is much better than we ever realised. In other words, count your blessings. Christmas is drawing near, and at all times right from childhood the Christmas season has always been a time for rejoicing with me, and I am trying to pass that rejoicing over to everyone whom I meet.
>
> It was very pleasing to know that you had some rain and on that small area the grass has responded and there is some green shoot there. Even if the grasshoppers do take a share out of it, that will be a start when the rain comes. We will get good rain, and perhaps sooner than you imagine, so let us give thanks and praise to the Lord for all the blessing that is to come and which has already come.

> PS. Dear Aubrey,
>
> Do not overdo yourself in trying to remove the sheep. Your life is worth more than all our sheep in Australia, so take the matter steady and be careful, think before acting.
>
> Rain is the most important, and I still see that we are going to get good rain. So don't get despondent.

Cousin Jenny remembered: 'When Grandad was in his 80s and staying with us, my brother Douglas was considering the purchase of *Ballygar* near Aramac. He rang to get Grandad's advice. As it was a desert place I know what the advice would have been, although I was not privy to the conversation.'

Grandad's possible advice is expressed in his eldest son Eric Back' memoir:

> Dad bought a desert protperty called *Rocklea*, south of Lochnagar, a siding on the Central Line between Jericho and Barcaldine. It proved to be a poor place, but then Dad had no experience of western land, but he learned from that experience.

WA wrote of his blunder of buying *Rocklea* and difficulties in selling it, making a tremendous effort to interest buyers in Victoria and Sydney:

> It almost gives me a headache now to think how much I worked. And wasted effort, and yet unexpectedly Sutherland and Reneck, (when they helped me untruck my first Dodge car which I had railed up to Barcaldine for Ellem) told me that they had £1000 in cash. I conceived the idea that they were my only buyers. It was a matter of making the best job I could with them, as I was completely beaten and would not have been able to get out waiting for any buyers coming through an agent, or effort on my part, looking to these distant hills for buyers.

1974 FLOODS

ENCIRCLED BY LOOPING RIVER, St Lucia has long been vulnerable to floods. From the outset of Western settlement, the early explorer John Oxley noted signs of past flooding when *en route* to Goodna. Eight major floods are recorded before 1890, when a dozen St Lucia families took refuge with neighbours who lived on higher ground. Similar to 1974, three cyclones within a two-week period caused the worst flood on record during 1893; three floods in February of that year caused 35 deaths.

Many lessons were learned—and forgotten—from earlier floods. The University buildings and colleges were designed with reference to the records of the Great Flood of 1893 and escaped deluge. The 1974 flood covered only the low lying areas of St Lucia, but included The Esplanade, where WA Back's office was located, as well as Hillside Terrace, Sandford Street, Brisbane Street, Guyatt Park and the Golf Links.

On Australia Day, 26 January 1974, torrential post-cyclone rain flooded Brisbane, and the low-lying areas of St Lucia that were encircled by the river curves were inundated. On 29 January, *The Courier Mail* printed an aerial view of the University headed 'Island University'. Two hundred St Lucia homes were inundated. (Condensed from Peter Brown, *Droughts, Floods Heritage Listings and Houses*, St Lucia History Group Paper 16, 2017.)

Although the house perched high above the river, the Office directly behind on The Esplanade did not escape. But WA found a bright side even in the disaster of the worst local flood in contemporary records:

We receive God's blessings daily, but very often we do not seem to realise it fully and give thanks. However, when floods, fires and other disasters happen to us we can then see how well we have been cared for in the past.

We are very high up, but when the river could not carry the large volume of water it spread out and sent water in all directions... A rise of another 20 foot drowned everything underneath our office—covered a car, penetrated into the strongroom where office records have been stored dating back 45 years. Many other valuables were spoilt and we had two truckloads taken to the rubbish dump to be burnt.

We are very happy to be on a dry floor in the office and praise the Lord from saving us from a flood on the top floor of this building where our latest records are kept.

All the family sheep stations have had over 30 inches of continuous rain, the gullies and little creeks have become inland lakes and by now nobody can ride or walk over the ground as it is waterlogged. We cannot ascertain how the sheep and cattle have fared but losses could be severe. Fences no doubt have been washed down. We cannot assess our losses until it dries up...

God knows all about it so we can give thanks glorify our Lord who watches over us, and if we submit ourselves to the will of God, all things will be well.

All things work together for good to them that love God.

DO IT NOW

Here I am facing a manuscript so large that it daunts me. How to piece the jigsaw bits together? I skulk away into petulant self-pity. A friend, supporting me in my moaning, emails: 'Just do it.' That pulls me up short. That was Grandad's motto. Or 'Do it now.'

Grandad, how can you make it all sound so easy? You were the ultimate multi-tasker. As I try to juggle all my work I wonder. How did you make sense of it all? Of course, you had a secretary and business partners. He speaks sternly now:

–'Do it now' I always say and that motto has served me well over the years. That, and my faith in the Good Lord who never failed me. Though many harvests did. Drought, pestilence… ah, the plagues of grasshoppers and mice, the like of which we never saw back in Finland. Though, life was tough there also, there's no denying it.

My family battled with nature in western Queensland. The sheep became fly-blown, were bogged in the puny water holes and bore drains—such shallow water, yet they had so little strength to pull themselves out. Or sense, perhaps.

Grandad would say those artesian bores were a sign of the good Lord's provision, sending us water even in the desert. Hot, boiling water, red and rusty straight from the bowels of the earth. There's something primeval about it, especially to consider this area was covered by Inland Sea millennia before.

Other sayings were:

'Come gagga (go car) with your Grandpa.'

'The best is yet to come!' It was a favourite saying.

'Never do what others do, and you'll be ok.'

—Aha, there lies our nonconformist bent.

A recorded interview from 1960 shows that after almost a lifetime in Australia Grandad's English was fluent. However, he still confused 'what' for 'that' and made plural 'peoples' and 'advices.' His speech was coloured with words that I later realised were Swedish or adaptations of it, like 'drinka kaffee' then 'vaska diska' (wash the dishes). When I came to learn the language I discovered he'd invented others. The word *congerichuchin* for a get–together still lives in family usage. Little wonder that it was typical of my family to play with words.

GRANDMA CHRISTINA BACK

CLOSE FRIENDS AND FAMILY CALLED Grandma 'Teenie,' and spoke of her smile and laugh, her soft kindly nature. My cousin Kay reminisced: 'She was my favourite of two grandmothers but I never felt a close bond as it seemed we girls were just three among so many, not really having any concept at that age of the impartial and all-embracing love of God which parental love reflects. I remember one conversation we had about a vision she told me she had of angels flying through a garden and hearing them singing. Mostly however, her conversations were more down to earth, with constant warnings about evil men lurking in the shadows, waiting to pounce on unsuspecting folk. She gave the impression of being quite acquiescent of all Grandad's comings and goings—I don't know how she coped actually: he'd turn up with four or more men in tow and expect her to feed them at a moment's notice!'

Grandad told another cousin his only regret was that business took him away from Christina and the family when the boys were young.

DARK DAYS OF DEMENTIA

Even in the late 1950s, Grandma showed signs of the early stages of dementia. My most clear memory of Grandma is of her buttering fruity Dutch loaf for us to devour in the curved breakfast nook. A cousin remembers that it was mouldy, and that cold foods were stored in the oven and hot in the refrigerator.

Dementia was already apparent when in 1956, Grandad took his wife, Elwyn and Joan and their children on a Grand Tour to Europe. A photograph shows the family in a Venetian gondola. Cousin Jenny told that one of them accompanied Grandma everywhere in case she might become lost.

When my grandparents were no longer self-sufficient, they lived for about five years in a granny flat with their daughter Gloria and her family. Grandma was moved to intensive nursing care for a year before she died on 11 August 1970. Grandad visited her regularly and tried to maintain conversation even when she could barely respond.

His letters reveal the pain that his companion of over a half-century faded from him.

He shared his struggles on 12 October 1970, that in 1963 after they returned from a trip to Japan, he complained to his wife that he was distressed and troubled in his dreams:

> To my surprise Mum looked at me so steadfast and said: 'I used to get those dreams too and I prayed to God to relieve me from these distressing dreams.' And I remember us reading from St John's epistle 1:7. Mum was completely freed and saved from any distressing dreams. She could sleep soundly, when I was tossing about, mostly due to the problems of this world. But the evil one kept churning that up continuously, whereas I should have passed it all onto our Lord, who told us so definitely, 'Pass your burden upon me and I will sustain you.'
>
> Now, looking over these six or seven years as I have been holding Mum's hand and praying with her, all these things seem to have completely showed me God's doing. Mum was not only relieved of her distressing dreams but God took her soul in hand and relieved her from all thoughts, cares or any anxieties of this world. She could sleep and rest in peace and that is the peace which Jesus gives us through the Holy Spirit.
>
> Let me make another confession of my folly: I prayed that God would open the channels in her head so that she would be able to speak to us and I felt sure that God would be able to convey something wonderful to us.
>
> In other words, I was tempting God, whereas I should have joined in to praise God for what he was doing in revealing himself to us... Yes, I confess that I have prayed for things which were out of step with Our Lord in Heaven, but now I can rejoice to confess these follies to you, so that you will be able to place your full faith in God and leave it with him.

In turn, my own father visited my mother in the nursing home, railed at her imprisonment in the 'dratted chair' that restrained her from wandering and falling. How he fought to take her out for a drive to see the outside world! Which might be less of a tonic than he hoped. For decades, Mum was his eyes and ears and guardian angel. 'Look out, Aubrey, there's a truck.' 'Mind the ditch,' she would warn. Long trips caused migraines. Being driven by him was a nail-biting rollercoaster; he would look anywhere but the road, often cutting into the path of other drivers' right of way.

The trusty chauffeur-come-gardener Clive Stone drove my grandparents to their riverside holiday home at Brunswick Heads when she had reached the distressing stages of dementia, and was a shadow of her earlier self. Might this spark happy memories of family holidays, of canoe and boat rides, of picnics by the beach? A photograph of them in a boat captures the loneliness within a marriage where one partner has become a shadow, yet is still loved for the memories, the hope of some small communication. Grandad talks with her, his eyes search hers. Christina looks down, vacant, yet gives a half-smile. She knows his touch, his arm around her. They were married 62 years, had shared so many experiences together, the heady days of setting up homes together, travelling the world and length of Australia, raising a family.

–You loved photographs, yet there are few in the press, on *Trove*. That studio portrait that graced our piano back home showed your beaming round face in round spectacles, Grandma in her pearls. In my memories, you always wore a suit, even in sweltering outback summers. So I was surprised when cousins sent me photographs of you boating and swimming in black bathers. They must have had more holiday fun with you than we did, being lower in the family pecking order.

I imagine your ache for a wife as she draws away. Times when loneliness yearns through nights, reaching for that other warm body and finding only cold sheets.

–*Christina was a faithful loving wife and good mother, she always made sure we had good food on the table, even when times were tough. Did she develop dementia because all those years I put her under the pressure of always travelling?*

–We live a peripatetic life, so I know how wearing that is, how it's bliss to stay in one place. Did Christina ever shake her head in bewilderment as you proposed new ventures? Or did she egg you on? I hear she sometimes reined in your wilder ideas?

–*Christina accepted without complaint the demanding life pressures thrust on her over the years. I miss her companionship she gave me over the decades.*

–You lived life in high gear, hurtling from one project to the next. To another exciting vision on the horizon that made the present seem less engrossing. Wally said of KJ that he tended to move on to another interest after he'd mastered each one, so perhaps you were similar. I see something of myself in this; and I hear again my husband's exasperated 'I just can't keep up with you and all your projects and ideas!'

Grandad, you stoked my entrepreneurial spirit. Life is never boring, chasing new whirlwinds across the horizon. I hope I will age as you did, still fresh, green and involved.

BIG HOUSE FOR SALE

Age curbs even an Action Man. When his wife slows her pace, so must he. Family rallies around, to move them into their care. Daughter Gloria and her husband Victor had already moved south, selling my father *Wilfred Downs*, and built their house a few blocks away towards the University. And so, the 'Big House' was listed for sale.

An undated PR brochure reassures that:

> The entire building has been meticulously maintained, both structurally and decoratively and stands ready for immediate possession. Here, indeed, is the opportunity of a lifetime for anyone seeking a residence in which the attributes of spaciousness and serviceability have been successfully merged with the exclusively different in both exterior and interior styling.

Eric Back wrote:

> There was some talk of selling it to the Japanese Government and Dad turned it down—he did not want their flag on his flagpole! After Mum died and the Americans had moved out, we wanted to sell the house to wind up the estate, but Dad, a good salesman, did not have his heart in it. He had a comfortable lounge chair in the lounge, the only furniture in the house, and he would sit there and think.

WEDDINGS AND FUNERALS

Grandad died peacefully on 2 April 1974. I missed his funeral, as we were out of range on our honeymoon. My last memory of him is his benign smile as he sat beside me in the extended family wedding photograph, as he said grace at the wedding breakfast a few weeks before. No doubt it gave Grandad great pleasure to have his few minutes' word to the family as well as to God.

Grandad sent us a King James Bible as a wedding present, with a cheque. His letter is cherished by the whole family as well as Antoni and myself, written with a real care for the future of his descendants. Each family function without his beloved Christina must have felt painful. 1974 had already been saddened by the death of his sister Sofia, the last of his siblings.

Eric wrote of his father's funeral in Mullumbimby.

> The Reverend Donald McClellan officiated. He was then Presbyterian moderator for Queensland, but more importantly he grew up knowing us all. His people lived at Wilson's Creek near Mullumbimby and he could speak with intimate knowledge of my father and mother. There are three graves together now. To the left is my Uncle KJ Back, then my mother and father. It is a peaceful place, the green valley of Mullumbimby Creek with the hills around. I hope it remains that way.
>
> Mr. Busing of Australian Estates Co., Brisbane, told Eric: 'I had to come, your father was a remarkable man, and this is the passing of an era.'

–Thank you, Grandad, for your inspiration that lives on for many future generations.

I have not located an Obituary but Joan Maxwell's daughter Kay Maxwell sent me a scan of family papers found in her possession, that she must have helped prepare. How many times might she have heard the story of her employer's choice of a new homeland?

> Getting off the train at Bangalow in January 1902, they found themselves in the Big Scrub.

'The parental guardian said: "Well, this is it. This is the Promised Land" and in the Australian vernacular, it is presumed, "Now it's up to you."

After a summation of WA's business and church contributions, she noted:

'It can be said that as a last act of loyalty, both he and his wife were interred in Mullumbimby cemetery.'

Her daughter Kay Maxwell adds a mystery of the missing will:

> When Mr Back passed away, there was a kerfuffle about the Will, which was kept in the safe at St Lucia. He had made a number of wills over the years, changing his mind about charities and bequests. Strangely, though, the only Will that could be found by Mr Nelson and the sons was one from some years earlier. None of the recent Wills seemed to have survived. There was much gossip about this and various family members contacted Mum and Clive privately to find out what, if anything, they knew. Mum told me that she knew that there were several Wills and codicils in the safe at one point but that she had no knowledge of what happened to any recent wills. Clive only knew that Mr Back had seen his solicitor and that he had witnessed documents but not what they contained. So, a mystery there.

WA Back died on 2 April 1974 just months after the January deluge that flooded the office, including the safe where the wills were kept. Were these destroyed in the floodwaters and thrown out?

From 1920 for the next 56 years, Vincent Nelson worked for WA in the office, and Eric Back wrote, 'he stuck with him through good and bad times until Dad died in 1974 and then he finalised his estate. Like the others, he was a very honest person.' Eric also noted that his father was an astute judge of land and of people. Many who worked with and for him retained loyalty through their lifetimes.

A LAST WORD

On 29 November 1993, WA Back's eldest son Eric died, soon after his 80th birthday. This prompted my mother Helen Back to send a letter to the family with memories of her father-in-law's last days with them. My copy is undated:

> We appreciate this time when we can come together in honour of Eric's eightieth birthday, especially as, in my mind we have looked up to him as the head of the clan since Grandad Back went to be with the Lord.
>
> Which brings me to the time in [March] 1974 when Grandad was out west and stayed with us at 'Hazelwood.'
>
> He was not, as in former times, interested in anything that was going on and what anyone was doing on the properties, but he stayed in his bedroom, just sitting in a chair with his mind far away.
>
> We tried all sorts of things to interest him. Would he like someone to read the paper to him, or for Aub to take him for a drive—to no avail.
>
> One morning Doug came and asked Grandad to come and have morning tea on the verandah with us. He dutifully came out and sat there, not even looking out to see the grass, or lack of it. He was mentally in another world.

> One day, he had not been at all well and that evening he sat in a chair with breathing so fast and heavy it frightened me. I kept sponging his face as the perspiration was pouring off it and prayed Lord don't let him die, don't let him die. I knew that the way his heart was pounding it could happen.
>
> The last evening Grandad was with us, Aub said something to him about prophecy and the future for us. That seemed to unlock the key to what was on his mind and for the first time he wanted to talk.
>
> He said: 'That's what is worrying me, that some of my grandchildren might not know the Lord Jesus as their Saviour and have to go through the Tribulation and be lost for eternity.'
>
> After he passed away, I felt that I should pass on to you his descendants, the concern he had for all of us.
>
> So, perhaps now is the time for each one of us to take stock and make sure of our eternal destiny that we may be not only with the Lord in Heaven, but also with Grandad Back.

End-time eschatology dogged my childhood and subsequent decades. Fear-mongering prophesies were updated after each date passed without the looming Tribulation; that we would face World War 3 in 2000 or 2016 or…

Would my own faith withstand the kind of tortures that boomed out via reel-to-reel tapes during my childhood, so insistent that a pillow on my head could not block them? My father buried barrels of 'benzin' and flour on our properties to safeguard against the imminent threat of invasions by red, yellow or multi-coloured foes. Before I boarded a flight for London on a path that would bring me perilously close to the mega-threat Russia, a brother gave me a copy of *The Late Great Planet Earth*. In Sweden and Finland, I came to understand the streak of paranoia that runs through our blood, courtesy of Russian domination and oppression. That warning: 'Russians have long memories.'

Even safely established at the other end of the world, did this fear cause my grandfather and his brother to fudge dates and arithmetic?

As a survivor of dire end-of-world-is-nigh predictions, conspiracy theories, negative and fearful religious fervour, I look for the positives that faith brings.

I thank Martin Luther for writing during the Reformation:

> Even if I knew that tomorrow the world would go to pieces, I would still plant my apple tree.

Let us all look up—and plant more trees.

WHAT DROVE THE MAN WHO BUILT THE 'BIG HOUSE'?

How can one encapsulate WA Back, a multi-faceted power house? Access to his voluminous correspondence around the country (indeed, the globe), illumines yet daunts in exposing the complexities of his projects, and his bright but short-lived ideas amid grandiose visions actually realised.

How much was WA Back driven by the need to prove himself to his father, to his family back home? Frustrated by distance, he put his wealth to help his country and compatriots rebuild after wars decimated. He packed (apparent) shiploads of provisions for post-wars Europe. In Finalnd, WA bought a town unit for his sister and niece and a car for his nephew Rolf. He sent a cheque to the Salvation Army to distribute gifts to Nykarleby Children's Home.

A primary goal of his 1924 travel to Finland was to encourage and persuade his brother and parents to emigrate. That was unsuccessful, but he sponsored a stream of Finns keen to migrate. Painting his adopted country as Utopia, he promised them all a bed and food when they arrived. By sponsoring land ballot applications for family, Finnish emigrants and colleagues, he expanded a kingdom of western sheep grazing properties.

Was he driven by the exciting opportunities offered by his new homeland? Or by the Migrant-Make-Good mentality? Grandad was honest about his urge to gain land:

> At first when I came to Australia I wanted selections, I wanted land, I wanted plenty of land. I soon got more than I could handle and more than what was good for me. I started to buy and subdivide, build and sell. I got more than I wanted. I started to sell for others, I got more business than I wanted and as soon as I got the desire to get out I think I got the very best man...The same thing could be said about selections in Queensland. I always got what I wanted and when I wanted to sell I could always get out.

Then he came to realise that it is better to give than to receive. That wealth cannot be taken to a next life. His philosopher brother Karl Johan Back put his broad spectrum global interest to writing treatises to solve the financial ills of the world—after WA rescued him from bankruptcy in 1928. So, too, Grandad delighted to support and rescue worthy causes.

These brothers were like two sides of a penny; one the multi-dealing capitalist; the other a socialist, dreamer and visionary who published books in a language he'd learned from a dictionary during his voyage to Australia.

WA was global and cosmopolitan, always reading and aware of events and trends around the world. Like his father Anders Back, he showed foresight and insights ahead of his time. Few could best Grandad in a business deal, yet some missionaries and reformed drunkard evangelists saw him as a soft touch. It may be that he found it hard to say no, but at heart he was a generous philanthropist who took pleasure to solve financial issues of supplicants. Yet he was not a trumpet blower, and his left hand did not know his right hand's generosity.

Thus, when I enlisted a library researcher to locate 'W. A. Back' in data bases, he asked, 'So, he wasn't a philanthropist or a patron, but just a rich businessman?' At the time it seemed so. Reading his correspondence to family, he was both of those but his giving was not often reported in the media.

As a patron of the arts, he sponsored his niece Perry Hart to study violin in Holland soon after World War II. He bought his wife a piano and lessons, encouraged Giuseppe ('Charles') Ive to branch beyond house painting and plastering, to paint murals. On his travels he bought glassware and sculpture, and took his family through galleries and museums, historical sites and landmarks.

One definite driver was his deep faith and his commitment to share it with others. His love of God and of people. Never mind language barriers, WA could relate and converse with anyone, high or low in society's pecking order. Like a chameleon, he could fit into any situation. Joan Maxwell told her daughter that WA was friendly with the Lord Mayor of London at one time. They met through wool business and struck up a friendship. They would correspond and telephone from time to time. Also that his wide ranging interests extended to phrenology at one point. Kay Maxwell remembers: 'He had a head at the office and book about it (which I read, of course).'

WA was driven to see his family settled on their own land and to help them succeed through droughts, floods and downturns.

A family man, he shone love and care for his myriad family. Wilhelm Anders Back would no doubt be delighted to know he has indeed exceeded the hundred descendants he hoped for. As the various branches of his offspring rallied to help me make a headcount and update the burgeoning family tree, it often seemed as challenging as counting stars. Our tally revealed WA had more than doubled his hope. At the time of writing, he has had 221 descendants in this sunburnt country so far from his birthplace of snow and ice and midnight sun.

BOOKS QUOTED OR CONSULTED

AUSTRALIA

Back, Eric, *William Andrew Back, Esq. and Mrs Back, from his arrival in Australia from Finland in 1902 until his death in 1974*. Brisbane, 1991, unpublished memoir. In both this and his handwritten 1924 journal, some punctuation has been added for clarity; some quotes have been shortened without ellipses for easier reading.

Bonetti, Ruth, *Burn My Letters: Tyranny to refuge*, Words and Music, 2016.

Bonetti, Ruth, *Midnight Sun to Southern Cross*, Words and Music, 2017.

Flett, Yvonne and Alick, *John James and Harriet Hart: A partial history of one family in England and Australia, 1856-1937, Lismore 1988*, unpublished memoir.

Hollingworth, Nicholas, *The Mullumbimby Sawmill*, Brunswick Valley Historical Society, Mullumbimby, 2012.

MacKinnon, Neta, *What They Did: Families of the Brunswick 1890-1950*, Brunswick Valley Historical Society, Mullumbimby, 1998.

Magub, Judy, *The History of St Lucia*, 1998.

Roberts, Beryl, *Naming Brisbane: Origins of Brisbane's Suburb and Locality Names*, 2013.

Siemon, Rosamund, *The Mayne Inheritance*, University of Queensland Press, 1999.

Spencer, Margaret, *John Howard Lidgett Cumpston, 1880–1954, A biography*. 1987, Tenterfield.

Thornton, Merle, *Bringing the Fight*, HarperCollins Australia, 2020.

Tsicalas, Peter, *Mullumbimby: Boom and Bust 1908-1928*, Brunswick Valley Historical Society, Mullumbimby, 2012.

Vader, John, *Red Gold: The tree that built a nation*, New Holland Press, 2002.

Walker, Shirley, *Roundabout at Bangalow*, University of Queensland Press, 2001.

FINLAND AND RUSSIA

Koivukangas, Olavi, *Sea, Gold and Sugarcane: Finns in Australia 1951-1947*, Turku, Institute of Migration, 1986.

Rayner, Richard, *The Cloud Sketcher*, HarperCollins, 2001. This novel tells of Finnish architect Esko Vaananen who read in 1901 newspaper *Hufvudstadsbladet* that 'An electric elevator, the first in Finland, has been installed in the new Diktonius Building on Aleksandersgaten in Helsingfors [Helsinki].' In *Midnight Sun to Southern Cross*, I surmised that WA Back was fascinated to experience this before emigrating to Australia.

Wall, Marketta, *To America: Hanko as Port of Departure for Emigrants*, 2013.

ARTICLES
CONTRIBUTIONS
WEB ARTICLES

Bonetti, Ruth. 'Munsala: St Lucia.' Contributor to Wilson, Kim. *Brisbane Art Deco: Stories of our Built Heritage*, Jubilee Studio, 2015.

Bonetti, Ruth. (2015): 'Two Finnish Migrants Down Under: An Australian bibliographical perspective', *Participation, Integration, and Recognition: Changing Pathways to Immigrant Incorporation*, Migration Studies C24, Turku, Institute of Migration, pp.167–176.

Bonetti, Ruth. (2015): 'Finland Through Australian Eyes', Siirtolaisuus-Migration Quarterly, Vol 1/2015, Turku, Institute of Migration, pp. 36–42.

Brown, Peter, 'Residential Development after the 1880s,' St Lucia History Group, February 2013.

Brown, Peter, 'St Lucia Industrial and Retail Development', St Lucia History Group Paper 15, 2017.

Brown, Peter, *Droughts, Floods Heritage Listings and Houses*, St Lucia History Group Paper 16, 2017.

Darbyshire, Andrew, 'Land Resumptions – UQ's move to St Lucia', brisbanehistorywordpress.com, April 2020.

McQueen, Humphrey, 'The "Spanish" Influenza Pandemic in Australia' 1919. (Originally published in 'Social Policy in Australia – Some Perspectives 1901–1975.' Edited by Jill Roe. Cassell Australia 1976).

MAD, 'About us', viewed April 2019, madparis.fr/en/about-us.

Unpublished promotion brochure from Back family archives.

'Australian rikkain suomalainen (Australia's Richest Finn)' An article ca. 1965 in uncited Finnish magazine. Author unknown.

COMMENTS AND ERRATA

WA's grandsons Bob Back and my brother Douglas used their light aircraft to muster sheep. My father learned to fly but did not gain his licence. WA did not have a private plane.

These 'farmlands' would have been in Western Queensland, rather than northern NSW. WA Back went in for Queensland land ballots and also partnered with friends and family members. In 1914 he and Walter Ellem drew a block called *Mellew*.

Numerical errors and misconceptions in 'Australia's Richest Finn' article include:

- WA arrived in Australia in January 1903, aged 16.5.
- WA and Christina married in November 1908.
- The family sailed from Sydney for Europe on 16 February 1924.
- Eric Back was born 16 December 1909 so was 13, turning 14 during the trip. (Grandad, it seems you are a fibber. Grandma had dementia, but your brain was sharp till your death. Did you, like KJ, cover tracks because of fear of repercussions by the Russian regime?)

During the 1940s WA organised a shipload of provisions to save Finnish people from famine. His office was strewn with sacks of flour and sugar, transferred into kilo-size calico bags. Sheep were canned for export.

UNPUBLISHED LETTERS

Letters from WA Back, dated 15 January 1947; 11 May 1954; 3 July 1969; 8 February 1974

NEWSPAPERS

The Brisbane Courier, 23 March 1893 p.5 c 5.

The Telegraph, 25 January 1962 p 33 c 3.

The Courier Mail, 26 February 1936 p. 18 c.1
　　'St Lucia—The Future Hamilton of the City—
　　Charming Sylvan Setting for New University'

The Courier Mail, 14 December 1949 p. 5
　　'Big St. Lucia homes scheme'

The Courier Mail, 19 April 1938 p. 5.
　　'Choice of Suburbs St. Lucia Fills the Role of A Cinderella'

The Courier Mail, 14 February 1952 p. 5
　　'St. Lucia Values New "Dress Circle"'

The Courier Mail, 3 March 1953, p. 5.
　　'St. Lucia's New Shops Are Nearly Completed'

The Sunday Mail, 18 February 1940, p. 14.
'Making a "Show Suburb"'

The Telegraph, 25 January 1962 p 33 c 3.

The Telegraph, 17 June 1951, p.5

⇒ CITATIONS ⇐

Image p 29: Coronation Park-StLucia-BCC plan 1913 S130 box435

State Archives Microfilm Z 3977 p 156 and File A/28567 op cit.

INDEX OF NAMES

Angel, Henry	91
Ashbury, GE	18
Back, Alan	137
Back, Anders Karlsson Ohls	35, 47, 53, 55, 151
Back, Aubrey	89, 102, 164
Back, Bob	4, 14-5, 184
Back, Christina née Hart	*throughout*
Back, Douglas	184
Back, (Nils) Edvard	47, 53, 55, 76
Back, Elwyn	11, 14, 64, 89, 116, 148, 162
Back, Eric William John	*throughout*
Back, Helen née Lord	128, 173
Back, Helmi 146	146
Back, Joan née Oakes	14, 116-7, 140, 162
Back, Johanna	47
Back, John	4, 15, 107, 119, 146
Back, Karl Johan ('KJ')	*throughout*
Back, Nils Edvard	47, 53, 55, 76
Back, Rolf	35, 76, 177
Back, Sanna	47, 55
Back, Sofia	53, 47, 55
Back, Wilhelm Anders (WA, Will, Billy, William Andrew)	*throughout*
Baker and Nicol, Managers	18

Bartlett, Jane	4, 118, 191
Bobrikov, Governor General Nikolai	33, 52–3
Bonetti, Antoni	35, 49, 169, 192
Browning, Arthur	122
Browning, Robert Elias ('Bob')	116, 122, 125
Bryce, Jack	4, 24
Bryce, Michael	4, 24–7, 120, 191
Bryce, Quentin	24
Carmichael, JH	18
Cass, John	51
Castrén, Jonas	52
Cramphorn, ER	23, 125
Crisp, Quentin 51	51
Cumpston, Dr John Howard Lidgett	85, 182
Cumpston, Dr Phillip	85, 191
Darbyshire, Andrew	73, 87, 183, 191
Day, Archie	60
Doyle, Edward Joseph	17–9
Doyle family	18
Ellem, Betty (Elizabeth) née Back	4, 191
Ellem, Walter	184
Fitzgerald, F. Scot	37
Ford, Leighton	151
Fors, Ellen	143
Francis, Kay née Hart	192
Gailey, Richard	72
Graham, Billy	151
Groszmann, Carl, *aka* Carl Keats	126
Hagman, Lucina	135
Hällsten, Judge and wife Betty	52
Hart, Fanny Elizabeth and Elsie May	47

Hart, Inez,	57
Hart, John James	80, 181
Hart, Perry	179
Hawken, Roger	109
Heikel, Rosina	135
Henry, Nurse CA	18
Hollingworth, Joe and Nicholas	76, 83, 181
Holm, Alice	54
Holm, Anna Sanna, née Back	53, 75
Holm, Erik Johan (Nyholm)	75
Holm, Wally	47, 53-5
Houseman, Gloria née Back	18, 120, 162, 167
Houseman, Kay	4, 120, 151, 161, 191
Houseman, Victor	32, 167
Hultin, Tekla	135
Isles, Love and Co	72
Ive, Giuseppe and Maria	10, 25, 126, 179
James, Frank	83
Keats, Colin	126
Keats, Rose	136
Kellas, Dr	68, 79
Kipner, Nat and Steve	126
Kohnke, Roy	138
Kokko, Urpo	39
Lang, Reverend John Dunmore	72
Lessing, Doris	135
Lockings, Harriet	80
Luther, Martin	153, 175
Mallum, G	18
Maxwell, Joan née Attewell	9, 32, 35, 116, 128, 136, 142, 170, 179
Maxwell, Kay	9-10, 108, 116, 125, 136, 142, 149, 170, 179

Mayne, Dr James	73, 86, 99, 182
Mayne, Mary Emelia	73, 86
McClellan, Reverend Donald	169
McInnis and Manning	18, 20
Melbourne, Professor	19
Millin, N	23, 125
Mörne, Arvid	52
Morrison, John	97
Mountcastle, Mrs	138
Nathan, Sir Matthew	18
Nelson, Colleen	32, 149
Nelson, EV 'Vincent'	18, 32, 95, 108, 149, 170–1
Newton-John, Olivia	126
Offner, GF and VJ	18
Ohls, Olof Olofsson	32
Oxley, John	157
Pitt, Son and Badgery	67
Redhead, Mr	132
Rees, Lloyd	100
Reville, Sub-inspector James and Mrs C	91–2
Roberts, Henry	118
Runeberg, Johan Ludvig	52
Seamens, C	18
Soutar, Arthur Henry	83
Starky, Jenny nee Back	4, 11, 14–5, 60, 117
Starr, Ringo	126
Stone, Clive	126, 140, 164, 170
Stone, Norma	126, 140
Svedberg, Anders	51–2
Swartze, Buchanan and Co 98	98
T.M. Burke Pty Ltd	17

Thornton, Merle	140–1, 182
Tierney, Ms MM	18
Topelius, Zacharias	52
Tsar Nicholas II	33, 52
Turner, Reverend Vernon	152
Voller, Ronald	24
Walker, Albert	93–5, 97
Wehl, Dawn, née Back	14, 151
Wilson, William Alexander	71

ACKNOWLEDGMENTS

'Why don't you write a book about Grandad?' family members urged, surprised that he played second fiddle to his black sheep brother in the first book of the trilogy, *Burn My Letters*. 'Because KJ has such a gripping story,' I responded.

But WA Back is squarely centre-stage in *Midnight Sun to Southern Cross*.

After which I heeded my great-grandfather's advice to his sons: 'This is your land now; forget Finland.' But the discovery of heritage has illumined my life and still haunts my heart and mind. When I decided to focus a book on Grandad with St Lucia as the pivot, I sought fresh material, rather than cut and paste relevant sections from *Midnight Sun*. It is inevitable that some material is replicated but I am grateful to those who offered fresh insights, memories and information. Foremost of those is Kay Maxwell, who my grandfather adored since he met this one-week old baby in hospital.

Thank you to Michael Bryce and his son Jack Bryce; Jane Bartlett; cousins Jen, John, Bob, Kay, Julie and Betty.

I am grateful to Dr Philip Cumpston who shared a memoir about his grandfather.

Thanks are due to Andrew Darbyshire of St Lucia History Group who shared maps and papers, and after a beta read, asked leading questions.

Thank you to my supportive writing buddy Debbie Terranova for further beta reading, insights, and suggestions. And to Dr. Peter Fenoglio for another luminous cover, to Michael Bretherton for drawing maps.

The undated, uncited Finnish article was translated by Camilla Ayala.

Graham and Denyse Back kindly shared the photograph of a young WA and Kay Francis images of Christina Hart.

Thank you Rebekah Robinson of Beckon Creative, for your enthusiastic embracing of Art Deco fonts, motifs and styles. For enduring multiple changes and back flips.

I am blessed that Anne Hamilton agreed to not only edit but also prepare the manuscript for publication.

My soul-mate Antoni Bonetti AM read and commented on the manuscript and ran the home and kitchen for two months while I was locked down with eyes glued to my computer screen.

ABOUT THE AUTHOR

Ruth Bonetti is a third generation Finland Swede Australian who grew up in the arid Queensland outback, intrigued by the strange-accented relatives she met on holidays near Byron Bay and on visits to 'The Big House' in St Lucia.

She preferred Mozart to hillbilly music, books to horses. Ruth's gift for classical music became a passport to the world.

Destiny led her to live in Sweden, directly across the Gulf of Bothnia from her grandfather's birthplace in Finland, where she researched the stories told in this trilogy.

Ruth is author/editor of a dozen publications about music, education and performance, five through Words and Music and two with Oxford University Press.

She is a Fellow of the Migration Institute of Finland where she presented a conference paper in 2014, published in *Participation, Integration, and Recognition: Changing Pathways to Immigrant Incorporation*. Ruth Bonetti has published in the Institute quarterly journal, *Siirtolaisuus-Migration Quarterly*.

Connect with Ruth Bonetti

Website: ruthbonetti.com

Email: ruth@ruthbonetti.com

Facebook: facebook.com/RuthBonetti

KJ Back has his own Facebook page: facebook.com/BurnMyLetters

See reviews at Amazon.com and Goodreads.com—and feel free to add your own comments.

OTHER BOOKS BY RUTH BONETTI

Other books in the *Midnight Sun to Southern Cross* Trilogy

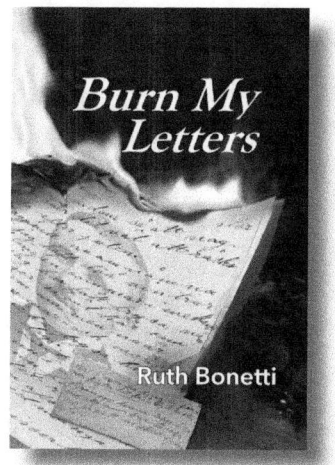

Book 1 of the Midnight Sun to Southern Cross Saga

Burn My Letters: Tyranny to Refuge

ISBN: 978-0-9875442-2-3

Winner, Omega Writers Nonfiction Caleb Award 2017

At the end of the 19th century Finland is a dark and repressive place. Pacifist and political dissenter Karl Johan Back is conscripted to fight for the Russian despots that occupy his country. In 1899 he flees to an untamed land on the far side of the world. Finding refuge on ridges overlooking the Byron Bay lighthouse in northern New South Wales, he plants orchids and grows lush tropical fruit.

Intrigued by her 'black sheep' great-uncle, Ruth Bonetti pieces together the motives that propelled his flight. Along the way she discovers much about her own voyage of self-discovery.

Finnish relatives share a treasure-trove of letters that provide answers to the many questions raised by Karl Johan's quest for freedom. Why did Russian military police pursue him as far as Suez? Why did he publish under a pen-name?

And, most intriguing of all, why did he implore his family to burn his letters?

Available at www.ruthbonetti.com

Reader reviews:

I absolutely loved *Burn My Letters*. I appreciated it was based on a true story. It took hold of my imagination. Some moments I wept a little, then later giggled, then held my breath in anticipation of the outcome of another adventure.

– Jenny Bardy-Back

This lovely book touches my heart deeply. It is a history of lives disrupted by famine and wars at the beginning of the twentieth century. Ruth Bonetti's first book (*Burn My Letters*) and also the second book, gives insight into how the destiny we choose for ourselves will affect those around us, and how trauma can be carried across generations. Can we understand ourselves without understanding where we originate from?

–Annika Wiklund-engblom

There is nothing dull about this historical search, from the start I was drawn into the story, entertained, amused, challenged and moved.

A timely book looking at the challenges of a political refugee, his efforts to find refuge in a new land (Australia) and the contributions he and his family have made in building our nation.

–Jeanette O'Hagan

Beautifully told with occasional photographs and diagrams, this is a rich treasure trove for future generations.

—Anne Hamilton

Ruth's writing is cohesive and easy to read. It capably supports the delightful ebb-and-flow of interesting situations, dramatic overtones, curious characters, evocative imagery and collective wisdom.

– Mazzy Adams

An excellent, challenging book. For anyone not only interested in European history but Australian stories of refugees who arrived here years ago, this is a must read.

– Mary Hawkins

These historical identities came alive for me, staring back from the pages, conferring their fears and despair, dreams and determination.

K.J. is a likeable dreamer, introspective, yet passionate about his family and country. I was inspired by the quoted passages from his work, and enjoyed the 'exchanges' between the author and her great uncle.

—Adele Jones

I couldn't tear myself away when I started. Very little has been written about these past pioneers from the top of the world who left their countries to brave this new land. I travelled with them through the pages and felt their angst and joy. I recommend this as an interesting, informative and entertaining read.

—Rose (Goodreads.com)

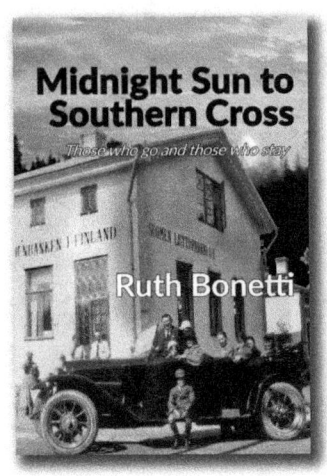

Book 2 of the *Midnight Sun to Southern Cross* Saga

Midnight Sun to Southern Cross: Those who go and those who stay

Winner, Queensland Family History Society, Family History Book Award, 2018

ISBN: 978-09875442-4-7

In the tradition of great family migration stories, *Midnight Sun to Southern Cross* continues the saga of the Back brothers' flight from Russian-occupied Finland to Australia as the nineteenth century turned into the twentieth.

From frozen Finland to the lush rainforests of northern New South Wales, to the dry and dusty sheep country of western Queensland, you follow the highs and lows of their new life under the Southern Cross.

It is an extraordinary tale of success, failure, hard work and dreaming. What drove the wheeler-dealer Wilhelm Anders Back, known as WA, to become in his time Australia's richest Finn? And what stirred his eccentric writerly elder brother Karl Johan, KJ, pacifist and political dissenter? What of those who stayed behind in Finland, and bravely struggled to oust the Russians from their homeland? This book, and its predecessor, *Burn My Letters*, are timely in the centenary year of Finnish Independence.

WA's granddaughter Ruth contrasts his and KJ's formative years in Finland with her own upbringing in outback Queensland. Her voyage of discovery and self-discovery uncovers research in Finland and Australia, and interweaves her own transformation from shy bush girl to speaker and musician.

Reader reviews:

This is not a dry family history, but a tale of adventure and momentous historical happenings. Ruth brings the past to life with her evocative descriptions, her dialogues and dramatic retellings, her imagined conversations with her ancestors. It is also a personal journey of discovery as Ruth delves deep into lives, emotions and motivations, including her own.

–Jeanette O'Hagan

Ruth tells it the way I remembered it all. All the way from Finland to Brisbane, Byron Bay, The North Coast of NSW around Lismore, Ocean Shores and much more. Particularly Hawken Drive, St Lucia, and their house. Just magic, similar to the one at Cavendish Road, Coorparoo. Well written!

–Bob Dix

I read *Burn My Letters* and *Midnight Sun to Southern Cross* with interest and fascination.

–Annette Whybird

I couldn't wait to read the second part of the family saga. Even if I wasn't connected to the Northern Land, which I am indirectly, I'd still be interested in the tale of these intrepid folk coming to our shores for new lives.

–Rose (Goodreads.com)

I really enjoyed this second book, even more than the first. I especially enjoyed the chapters around *'Finding Finland'*. I felt there was good balance in the way the characters were presented. As I read on, I thought often about the huge personal and research journey you must have been on to compile the story. This has dominated years of your life. Wow. Such tenacity. Congratulations.

–J.T. (Goodreads.com)

Additional books by Ruth Bonetti:

Don't Freak Out - Speak Out: Public speaking with confidence (Words and Music) Launched 2001, plus new editions.

Enjoy Playing the Clarinet (Oxford University Press, 1985; 2nd edition 1991)

Taking Centre Stage (Albatross Books, 1997)

Sounds and Souls: How music teachers change lives (Words and Music, 2013)

Confident Music Performance: Fix the fear of facing an audience (Words and Music, 2003, 2009)

Practice is a Dirty Word: How to clean up your act (Words and Music, 2002, 2009)

Clarinet Series 2 Grade Books 1-4, Editorial Consultant, Australian Music Examinations Board.

'Two Finnish Migrants Down Under: An Australian Biographical perspective', *Participation, Integration, and Recognition: Changing pathways to Immigrant Incorporation*, Institute of Migration, Turku, Finland, 2015 (conference paper).

'Munsala, St Lucia', *Brisbane Art Deco: Stories of our Built Heritage*. Brisbane, Jubilee Studio, 2015 (contributor).

www.ingramcontent.com/pod-product-compliance
Lightning Source LLC
Chambersburg PA
CBHW071917290426
44110CB00013B/1391